An Introduction to Buddhism

SECOND EDITION

 SGI-USA

For more information about Nichiren Buddhism and a
free electronic copy of *An Introduction to Buddhism*,
please visit the SGI-USA website:
www.sgi-usa.org

ISBN: 978-1-935523-98-7

Cover source background: www.gettyimages.com
Cover and interior design: Lightbourne, Inc.

Published by the SGI-USA
606 Wilshire Blvd.
Santa Monica, CA 90401
www.sgi-usa.org

21 20 19 18   4 5 6 7 8

Contents

Preface

Can Buddhism help improve your life? What are the keys to a successful prayer? What does Nam-myoho-renge-kyo mean? What is karma, and is it something you change for the better? In *An Introduction to Buddhism*, you will find the answers to these and many other questions.

Studying Buddhism and embracing its empowering concepts help us develop our faith and establish a regular daily practice. But finding time to study isn't always easy, so we can all benefit from some inspiration on why Buddhist study is so crucial. Hence we've chosen to begin this book with some encouraging words of Daisaku Ikeda, the president of the SGI. He succinctly explains how understanding the Buddhist viewpoint—an understanding gained from study—can help you develop deeper joy and appreciation in your everyday life.

You can read the subsequent five chapters in order or feel free to jump around and read whatever piques your interest. Each chapter is self-contained and offers great insights into this Buddhist practice.

The selected topics will appeal to both new and longtime practitioners, and the book itself will serve several purposes as:

* A catalyst for more in-depth discussions about core Buddhist ideas and historical events.
* A reference for presentations at SGI-USA study and discussion meetings.
* The official study material for the SGI-USA Introductory Exam, administered through the organization from time to time.

No matter how long you've practiced, we trust this book will allow you to discover new ideas, deepen your understanding and inspire you to learn even more about the vast realm of Nichiren Buddhism and how it can bring happiness to you and your friends.

SGI-USA Study Department

Study in
Nichiren Buddhism

The following are excerpts from
SGI President Ikeda's writings.

A member once said to second Soka Gakkai president Josei Toda that though she found lectures on Nichiren Daishonin's writings very moving, by the time she got home, she had forgotten what was said. Mr. Toda replied with a reassuring smile: "That's all right. No matter how many times you forget, if you keep attending and listening to such lectures, something indelible will invariably remain in your life. That intangible accumulation will eventually become a great source of strength for you."

The important thing is to continue making efforts to study the writings of Nichiren Daishonin, even a little every day. Taking the entrance exam is the starting point of your lifelong pursuit of Buddhist study. There's no need to feel anxious about or pressured by the exam. It is OK if you don't understand certain points or concepts right away. When you do finally come to grasp them, your joy will be all the greater. (February 25, 2011, *World Tribune*, p. 5)

Studying to deepen our understanding of Buddhism is part of our practice for attaining Buddhahood. It is something that goes beyond merely trying to pass an exam. I hope that our youth division members will ponder the significance of this fact, and challenge themselves in their studies with courage, wisdom, tenacity and perseverance, in a way that is true to themselves as youth and as young successors of the Soka Gakkai.

Our noble efforts to study and practice the great teaching of Nichiren Buddhism will definitely bring us boundless and immeasurable benefits that also will flow on to our descendants. (December 16, 2011, *World Tribune*, p. 8)

Faith means strong conviction and belief—namely, absolute faith in the Gohonzon. Practice means chanting for the happiness of ourselves and others, and sharing Nichiren Daishonin's teachings with others. Study means engraving in our lives the Daishonin's writings, which pulse with his powerful spirit to lead all people to enlightenment and to withstand any hardship to propagate the Law.

Making continuous efforts in faith, practice and study is the most fundamental way to develop our movement for kosen-rufu.

Faith is for a lifetime, and study enables us to deepen our faith for that purpose.

Through Buddhist study, it is important that we gain a deeper sense of joy and conviction in the greatness of Nichiren Buddhism; that we develop a more profound attitude toward reciting the sutra morning and evening, and chanting Nam-myoho-renge-kyo; that we are able to recall the Daishonin's teachings and summon forth invincible courage when we encounter problems or difficulties; and that we come to advance with pride and confidence, knowing that we possess a noble mission to strive for kosen-rufu in unity with our fellow members. (December 2, 2011, *World Tribune*, p. 5)

The essence of Buddhist practice, unchanged since Nichiren's time, lies in fellow practitioners gathering to study Nichiren's writings, deepen their faith and renew their determination to carry out kosen-rufu and their own human revolution.

The Daishonin often urged his followers to read his letters together. For instance, he writes, "I want people with seeking minds to meet and read this letter together for encouragement" ("Letter from Sado," *The Writings of Nichiren Daishonin*, vol. 1, p. 306). And in another writing, addressed to followers closely acquainted with each other (the lay nun of Ko and the lay nun Sennichi), he writes, "Since you two are of the same mind, have someone read this letter to you and listen to it together" ("Letter to the Lay Nun of Ko," WND-1, 595).

The model of friends in faith gathering and reading Nichiren's letters aloud, studying their significance, encouraging one another and resolving to triumph in life by following his teachings is exactly what today's discussion meetings are about. Discussion meetings are Soka Gakkai activities that, brimming with friendship, goodwill and inspiration, are in complete accord with the formula outlined in Nichiren's writings. (September–October 2010 *Living Buddhism*, pp. 13–14)

Second Soka Gakkai president Josei Toda said that there were two kinds of Buddhist study—one that delved into the teachings academically and the other that explored the teachings through faith. United by the deep bonds of the oneness of mentor and disciple, Mr. Toda and I waged all our struggles for kosen-rufu based on Buddhist study that explored the teachings through faith. That is why the Soka Gakkai has triumphed. Through studying the Daishonin's teachings while actively exerting themselves in efforts to advance kosen-rufu, our members have achieved one brilliant victory after another. (December 16, 2011, *World Tribune*, p. 5)

Nichiren's writings are a wellspring of hope, a melody of joy, a jeweled sword of courage, a banner of justice and a beacon of peace. They are teachings for mentors and disciples in faith to achieve everlasting victory.

The Daishonin cites a passage from *The Words and Phrases of the Lotus Sutra* by the Great Teacher T'ien-t'ai, "One accepts [the Lotus Sutra] because of one's power of faith and continues because of one's power of constant thought" ("The Difficulty of Sustaining Faith," WND-1, 471). To accept and uphold the correct teaching of Buddhism is the noblest commitment of all.

When we learn the sound life philosophy of Nichiren Buddhism, we have nothing to fear. When youth stand up with the resolve to establish the correct teaching for the peace of the land, they are invincible. Nothing can stop the advance of our gathering of ordinary people who have engraved the Daishonin's writings in their hearts and are striving with powerful conviction in faith. (December 17, 2010, *Seize the Day*, p. D)

Study the writings of Nichiren Daishonin
and practice as they teach,
with a pure heart,
regarding today's efforts
as a cause for eternal happiness.

(September–October 2010 *Living Buddhism*, p. 12)

Buddhist Concepts

Some religions place primary emphasis on faith. Others strongly stress practice or acts of kindness. Some promote philosophical inquiry, while others discourage it, leaving such pursuits to religious professionals. Nichiren Buddhism encourages a dynamic balance of faith, practice and study.

Nichiren Daishonin writes: "Exert yourself in the two ways of practice and study. Without practice and study, there can be no Buddhism. You must not only persevere yourself; you must also teach others. Both practice and study arise from faith" ("The True Aspect of All Phenomena," *The Writings of Nichiren Daishonin*, vol. 1, p. 386).

Faith

Faith in Buddhism is belief in our own vast potential and the limitless potential of all people to establish lives of unshakable happiness. This belief is expressed in the practice of chanting Nam-myoho-renge-kyo, the Mystic Law, the fundamental Law permeating our lives and the universe (see pages 11–15).

Nichiren Daishonin faced numerous persecutions and hardships in the course of establishing his teaching and triumphed in every instance. He inscribed the Gohonzon as an expression of his winning state of life, so that future generations could bring forth the same life condition (see pages 31–35). He writes, "I, Nichiren, have inscribed my life in sumi ink, so believe in the Gohonzon with your whole heart" ("Reply to Kyo'o," WND-1, 412).

The basis of Nichiren Buddhist practice is believing deeply that chanting Nam-myoho-renge-kyo to the Gohonzon enables all people to reveal their innate Buddhahood. When we chant to the Gohonzon with faith, we fuse our lives with the Mystic Law and reveal the wisdom, courage, compassion and all that is necessary to overcome any hardship and to help those around us do the same. Nichiren tells us never to seek the Gohonzon or enlightenment outside our own lives (see "The Real Aspect of the Gohonzon," WND-1, 832, and "On Attaining Buddhahood in This Lifetime," WND-1, 3). Faith in the Gohonzon, therefore, means faith in the tremendous power and nobility inherent in our lives and the lives of others. Buddhist practice and study strengthen our faith. And the stronger our faith, the more benefit and growth will result from practice and study.

Practice for Oneself and Others

Faith often begins as a simple expectation of how Buddhism can help improve one's life. With consistent practice, this expectation develops into conviction. Nichiren Buddhist practice consists of practice for oneself and practice for others. These are compared to the two wheels of a cart; both are necessary for the cart to move ahead properly.

Practice for oneself refers to chanting and reciting the sutra on a daily basis. We do this to bring about and maintain the high life condition necessary to establish enduring happiness. Practice for others constitutes teaching people about Nam-myoho-renge-kyo and helping them establish their Buddhist practice and thereby create fulfilling lives. SGI activities aimed at further spreading Nichiren Buddhism and its humanistic philosophy are also part of this practice for others.

Nichiren writes, "Single-mindedly chant Nam-myoho-renge-kyo and urge others to do the same; that will remain as the only memory of your present life in this human world" ("Questions and Answers about Embracing the Lotus Sutra," WND-1, 64). The happiness we create through chanting is eternal, transcending the boundaries of birth and death.

By chanting Nam-myoho-renge-kyo and teaching others, we break through the negativity that keeps us from becoming absolutely happy. When we practice consistently, we continue to strengthen and develop ourselves, paving the way for a joyful and rewarding life.

Study

Study in Nichiren Buddhism means reading Nichiren's writings in order to correctly understand the Buddhist teachings and apply them more effectively in our lives. By deepening our knowledge of the teachings of Nichiren Buddhism, we strengthen our confidence and conviction and learn what it means to practice correctly. Nichiren states: "Both practice and study arise from faith. Teach others to the best of your ability" ("The True Aspect of All Phenomena," WND-1, 386). By continually studying and seeking the correct Buddhist teaching, we can avoid the pitfall of forming shallow views based on personal opinion or the incorrect interpretations of others. To be misled by such things will prevent us from fully bringing forth our Buddha nature and enjoying the true benefit of our practice. Therefore, we also study the words and examples of the three

Soka Gakkai presidents—Tsunesaburo Makiguchi, Josei Toda and Daisaku Ikeda—who have fully applied and validated the teachings of the Daishonin in this modern age.

Second president Josei Toda once remarked, "Reason gives rise to faith; faith, in turn, seeks reason; reason thus gained elevates faith; and faith thus elevated further deepens reason." In other words, as we deepen our understanding of Nichiren Buddhism, we can establish stronger faith. And with stronger faith, we will seek further understanding of Nichiren Buddhism.

In the course of our lives, we will certainly experience difficulties and at times may wonder, *If I'm practicing Buddhism, why do I have this problem?* As we deepen our faith through study, we come to see the opportunity within problems and obstacles and fortify our ability to overcome them. "Buddhist study," President Ikeda says, "provides us with a great philosophy that serves as a compass to traverse the stormy and perilous seas of life. The more solid our foundation in Buddhist study, the stronger our faith will grow" (December 9, 2005, *World Tribune*, p. 2).

Through deepening our understanding of Nichiren Buddhism, we can resolve our doubts and continue toward establishing a state of unshakable happiness.

Nam-myoho-renge-kyo

Friends or acquaintances curious about Nichiren Buddhism often ask what Nam-myoho-renge-kyo means. This is a very important and difficult question, one that cannot really be answered in a brief or cursory way. It's best to consider what Nichiren Daishonin himself said about this.

Nichiren tells us, "There is no true happiness for human beings other than chanting Nam-myoho-renge-kyo" ("Happiness in This World," *The Writings of Nichiren Daishonin*, vol. 1, p. 681). He goes on to explain that while life is naturally filled with joy and suffering, ups and downs, there is a deeper and more enduring happiness. This he calls the "boundless joy of the Law" (WND-1, 681) that underlies and supersedes the cycles of temporary happiness and suffering all people experience.

He identified the chanting of Nam-myoho-renge-kyo as the means to establish a deep-seated, enduring and genuine happiness.

The Title of the Lotus Sutra

In his writings and recorded oral teachings, Nichiren Daishonin comments in detail and from various perspectives on the meaning of Nam-myoho-renge-kyo.

First, the title and essence of the Lotus Sutra, Shakyamuni Buddha's highest teaching, is Myoho-renge-kyo.

The Lotus Sutra's Sanskrit title is *Saddharma-pundarika-sutra*. The renowned fourth-century Buddhist scholar and translator Kumarajiva fully grasped the meaning behind the Lotus Sutra's title and translated it from Sanskrit into Chinese as *Miao-fa-lien-hua-ching*. In Japanese, these Chinese characters are pronounced Myoho-renge-kyo.

To Nichiren, this phrase signified something far beyond being simply the title of a Buddhist text. It was the principle, or Law, at the very heart and core of the sutra's teaching. He added *nam* to Myoho-renge-kyo and set forth the chanting of Nam-myoho-renge-kyo as the practice to accord one's life with this Law, which he identified as the law of life itself.

Nam comes from the Sanskrit word *namas*, which was translated in Chinese and Japanese as meaning "to dedicate one's life." "Dedication," Nichiren says, means "dedication to the principle of eternal and unchanging truth" (*The Record of the Orally Transmitted Teachings*, p. 3). And "life" indicates that, when dedicated to this principle, our lives become based on wisdom that perceives that truth and functions in response to any changing circumstance.

What does this mean to us? When we live our lives based on Myoho-renge-kyo, the Mystic Law—the ultimate truth or law of life—we exhibit the wisdom to deal effectively with any situation, creating the most valuable outcome.

Nichiren says, "We may also note that the *nam* of Nam-myoho-renge-kyo is a Sanskrit word, while *myoho*, *renge*, and *kyo* are Chinese words" (OTT, 3). He suggests here that the teaching of Nam-myoho-renge-kyo is not limited to any one language or culture. For Nichiren, in thirteenth-century Japan, Sanskrit represented the cultures and languages of the Western world, while Chinese represented those of the East. As a merging of the languages of East and West, Nam-myoho-renge-kyo is a phrase that represents the voices of all humanity, a universal teaching.

Nichiren practiced this principle exactly as taught in the Lotus Sutra and spread it for the happiness of all human beings. In doing so, he encountered harsh persecutions, as the Lotus Sutra predicted would befall its votary, or correct and devoted practitioner. In this sense, he "read" the Lotus Sutra with his entire life, fully realizing a state of oneness with the essential law or truth of life, Myoho-renge-kyo. This is what he means when he writes, "The Buddha's will is the Lotus Sutra, but the soul of Nichiren is nothing other than Nam-myoho-renge-kyo" ("Reply to Kyo'o," WND-1, 412).

Because he was the first to manifest this Law in his life for the sake of all people, Nichiren Daishonin is respected as the true Buddha of the Latter Day of the Law.

What Is the Meaning of Myoho-renge-kyo?

In brief, *myo* of *myoho* means "wonderful" or "mystic," and *ho* means "law," "principle," "teaching" or "phenomena." Together, *myoho* is translated as "Wonderful Law" or "Mystic Law." Nichiren Daishonin says: "*Myo* stands for the Dharma nature or enlightenment, while *ho* represents darkness or ignorance. Together *myoho* expresses the idea that ignorance and the Dharma nature are a single entity" (OTT, 4). *Myoho*, then, expresses both the enlightened nature of a Buddha and the deluded nature of an ordinary person, and the fact that they are essentially one.

While most Buddhist schools see a huge difference between a Buddha and an ordinary person, Nichiren aimed to erase any idea of separation between the two. For instance, in "The Heritage of the Ultimate Law of Life," he writes: "Shakyamuni Buddha who attained enlightenment countless kalpas ago, the Lotus Sutra that leads all people to Buddhahood, and we ordinary human beings are in no way different or separate from one another. To chant Myoho-renge-kyo with this realization is to inherit the ultimate Law of life and death" (WND-1, 216).

He also writes, "*Myo* represents death, and *ho*, life" (WND-1, 216). And in "On Attaining Buddhahood in This Lifetime," he writes, "*Myo* is the name given to the mystic nature of life, and *ho*, to its manifestations" (WND-1, 4). Hence, *myoho* is also the essence of life itself that is manifest while one is alive and continues in a latent state in death.

Renge, literally "lotus flower," also has a profound meaning in Nichiren Buddhism. Because the lotus produces both flower and seeds at the same time, it illustrates the principle of the "simultaneity of cause and effect." In other words, flower and seed, cause and effect, Nichiren says, are a "single entity" (OTT, 4).

Here, "cause" refers to the efforts or practice one carries out with the aim of becoming a Buddha, and "effect," to the actual attainment of Buddhahood. The simultaneity of cause and effect means that the very moment we chant Nam-myoho-renge-kyo with the intention of improving our lives, the life condition of Buddhahood, imbued with courage, compassion and wisdom, emerges within us and guides our actions.

The final character, *kyo*, Nichiren describes as the "words and voices of all living beings" (OTT, 4). *Kyo*, meaning "sutra" or "teaching," indicates the teaching the Buddha expounded with his voice. Nichiren explains, "The voice carries out the work of the Buddha, and this is called *kyo*, or sutra" (OTT, 4). This means that our voices when chanting or speaking to others about Nam-myoho-renge-kyo resonate with and stimulate the Buddha nature within us, within others and in our environment.

There are many other perspectives from which Nichiren explains the meaning and significance of Nam-myoho-renge-kyo. Most important, though, is to remember that it signifies dedicating our lives to the Mystic Law. Acting based upon that Law, we work for the happiness of ourselves and others.

Nichiren says that, while Nam-myoho-renge-kyo was known by Buddhist teachers of the past, they did not teach it to others or spread it widely. He writes: "Now, however, we have entered the Latter Day of the Law, and the daimoku [Nam-myoho-renge-kyo] that I, Nichiren, chant is different from that of earlier ages. This Nam-myoho-renge-kyo encompasses both practice for oneself and the teaching of others" ("On the Receiving of the Three Great Secret Laws," WND-2, 986).

What Should We Keep in Mind While We Chant?

In Nichiren Buddhism, action is most important. Only by taking action and applying our Buddhist practice to our day-to-day challenges can we demonstrate the real power of chanting Nam-myoho-renge-kyo. This becomes apparent through our character, our benefits and our victories in life.

Nichiren Daishonin says that in chanting, faith, or one's heart, is what is important (see "The Strategy of the Lotus Sutra," WND-1, 1000). This means to chant Nam-myoho-renge-kyo with firm conviction in our own limitless potential and that of others, determined to bring about our own happiness as well as the happiness of others just as Nichiren taught. When we do so, we will see clear proof of the power of the Mystic Law in our lives.

SGI President Ikeda states: "Nam-myoho-renge-kyo . . . directs us on a course to absolute victory. Nichiren Buddhism enables us to develop a serene life state of inner abundance pervaded by the noble virtues of eternity, happiness, true self and purity. Those who embrace faith in Nam-myoho-renge-kyo possess far, far greater wealth than those who have the most staggering fortunes or the most luxurious mansions. Nam-myoho-renge-kyo is the life and fundamental law of the universe. When we chant Nam-myoho-renge-kyo, we have nothing to worry about. The Daishonin's words are never false. The purpose of our faith and practice is to achieve happiness and victory in our lives. This is the reality of the Buddhism of Nichiren Daishonin, the one and eternal Buddha of the Latter Day of the Law" (March 5, 2010, *World Tribune*, p. 4).

Under President Ikeda's leadership, SGI members have been earnestly dedicated to kosen-rufu—the worldwide spread of Nam-myoho-renge-kyo—just as Nichiren Daishonin taught. As a result, they have been showing proof of its beneficial power for the sake of humanity on a global scale.

The Ten Worlds

Through examining the "Ten Worlds"—a classification of ten distinct states of life—we can get a clearer understanding of the dynamics of the Buddhist philosophy of the human condition and gain insight as to how to improve it.

The Ten Worlds are: the world of hell; the world of hungry spirits (also called hunger); the world of animals (animality); the world of *asuras* (anger); the world of human beings (humanity or tranquillity); the world of heavenly beings (heaven or rapture); the world of voice-hearers (learning); the world of cause-awakened ones (realization); the world of bodhisattvas; and the world of Buddhas (Buddhahood).

Among these, hell, hunger, animality, *asuras*, humanity and heaven are known collectively as the "six lower worlds" or the "six paths." The worlds of voice-hearers, cause-awakened ones, bodhi-sattvas and Buddhas are known as the "four noble worlds."

The idea of the six paths originates with the ancient Indian worldview that envisions six broad realms within which all living beings transmigrate through the repeated cycle of death and rebirth. Buddhism adopted this view. The four noble worlds indicate levels or states beyond the six paths that are achieved through Buddhist practice.

Sutras other than the Lotus Sutra often define these worlds as places inhabited by certain kinds of beings, or, in the case of the four noble worlds, by Buddhist practitioners. For instance, hell is viewed as a place of torment that exists underground, while Buddhas and bodhisattvas are believed to dwell in pure lands far from the ordinary realm of human beings.

But the Lotus Sutra overturns this way of thinking, teaching "the mutual possession of the Ten Worlds"—that each of Ten Worlds possesses the potential of all ten within itself. Rather than distinct realms, the Ten Worlds are conditions of life that everyone has the potential to experience at any time.

Nichiren Daishonin writes: "Neither the pure land nor hell exists outside oneself; both lie only within one's own heart. Awakened to this, one is called a Buddha; deluded about it, one is called an ordinary person. The Lotus Sutra reveals this truth, and one who embraces the Lotus Sutra will realize that hell is itself the Land of Tranquil Light" ("Hell Is the Land of Tranquil Light," *The Writings of Nichiren Daishonin*, vol. 1, p. 456).

What does this mean for us? From one perspective, though in one moment we may experience the misery characterized by the world of hell, in that same moment, through Buddhist practice, we can begin transforming our lives so that we can savor the deep, inexhaustible joy of the world of Buddhahood.

The World of Hell

The Japanese word for hell, *jigoku* (Skt *naraka*), suggests an "underground prison." Hell represents the basest human condition in which one is fettered by agony, completely lacking in freedom.

Nichiren writes, "Hell is a dreadful dwelling of fire" ("Letter to Niike," WND-1, 1026). If we consider hell as a potential state of life, it describes being so overwhelmed that our suffering seems to engulf us completely, like roaring flames. Nichiren also states, "Rage is the world of hell" ("The Object of Devotion for Observing the Mind," WND-1, 358). Rage, here, means desperation and resentment arising from the inability to quell misery, with no hope of respite from torment.

Hell is a state of life in which one feels that living itself is suffering and that whatever one sees or encounters causes more suffering. We could also say that in the world of hell we are controlled by destructive impulses. War, which embodies extremes of human misery, can be considered an expression of the world of hell.

The World of Hunger

The world of hungry spirits, or hunger, is characterized by over-whelming desires and the suffering that comes from those desires going unfulfilled.

The Japanese term *gaki* (Skt *preta*), translated as "hungry spirit" or "hungry ghost," originally referred to the dead. This is because the dead were thought to be in a constant state of starvation. The world of hunger is a condition in which our mind and body burn with constant intense craving.

Nichiren Daishonin writes, "The realm of hungry spirits is a pitiful place where, driven by starvation, they devour their own children" ("Letter to Niike," WND-1, 1026). He also says, "Greed is [the world] of hungry spirits" ("The Object of Devotion for Observing the Mind," WND-1, 358). To be hungry to the point of devouring one's own children is to be ruled by the misery of craving that knows no bounds.

Desire in itself is neither good nor bad. Without a sense of hunger when our bodies need nourishment, we would starve to death. Desires and wants can provide impetus for self-improvement, for human advancement. In the world of hunger, however, we are unable to use desires creatively. We become slaves to them and suffer as a result.

The World of Animals

The world of animals, or animality, is characterized by motivation based on immediate gain or loss rather than on reason or logic. Nichiren Daishonin says, "Foolishness is [the world] of animals" ("The Object of Devotion for Observing the Mind," WND-1, 358). When in the state of animality, one acts based on instinct or impulse, unable to distinguish between right and wrong, good and evil.

Nichiren also writes, "It is the nature of beasts to threaten the weak and fear the strong" ("Letter from Sado," WND-1, 302), and that the realm of animals is characterized by the need "to kill or be killed" ("Letter to Niike," WND-1, 1026). In the world of animality, people lack reason and conscience, seeing life as a struggle for survival in which they are willing to harm others to protect themselves. Unable to look beyond the immediate, they cannot plan for the future. Such a state of ignorance ultimately leads to suffering and self-destruction.

While Buddhism draws from ancient Indian tradition in associating this state of life with animals, in reality, animals can exhibit qualities, such as loyalty and selflessness, from which humans could gain by learning. And animals play an irreplaceable role in supporting human life. Human beings, on the other hand, can be capable of baseness and cruelty, such as seen in wartime, that surpasses anything in the animal world.

Because the worlds of hell, hungry spirits and animals all represent conditions of suffering, they are collectively known as the "three evil paths."

The World of Asuras

An *asura* is a contentious god or demon found in Indian mythology. One characteristic of those in the life state known as the world of asuras, also called anger, is a strong tendency to compare themselves with and a preoccupation with surpassing others. When they see themselves as superior to others, these people become consumed with arrogance and contempt. If, on the other hand, they encounter a person who seems clearly their superior, they become obsequious and given over to flattery.

People in the world of asuras often put on airs in order to impress others with their self-perceived greatness.

On the surface, those in this world may appear well-intentioned and civil, even humble. Inwardly, however, they harbor jealousy or resentment toward those they sense as better than them. This conflict between outward appearance and behavior and inner feelings and orientation makes those in the world of asuras prone to hypocrisy and betrayal.

This is why Nichiren Daishonin writes that "perversity is [the world] of asuras" ("The Object of Devotion for Observing the Mind," WND-1, 358). The Japanese word *tengoku*, translated here as "perversity," is composed of two characters meaning "to submit without revealing one's true intent," and "bent" or "twisted," respectively.

Unlike the three evil paths—the worlds of hell, hunger and animality—in which one is controlled by the three poisons (the fundamental human delusions of greed, anger and foolishness), those in the world of asuras display a stronger degree of self-awareness and control. In this sense, it could be considered a higher state than the three evil paths. Nevertheless, remaining in the condition of asuras ultimately gives rise to suffering and therefore constitutes, together with hell, hunger and animality, one of the "four evil paths."

Though the world of asuras is often called the world of anger, this does not mean it is characterized by rage or the tendency to lose one's temper. Rather, it suggests an abiding sense of contention or predisposition toward conflict arising from self-centered ambition.

The World of Human Beings

The world of human beings, or humanity, is a condition of composure and tranquillity. Thus, Nichiren Daishonin says, "Calmness is [the world] of human beings" ("The Object of Devotion for Observing the Mind," WND-1, 358).

One aspect of the world of humanity is the quality of reason that enables us to distinguish right from wrong and to make judgments based on that distinction. In this condition, a person also has a fair degree of self-control. "The wise may be called human, but the thoughtless are no more than animals" ("The Three Kinds of Treasure," WND-1, 852), writes Nichiren.

To remain in this state of humanity, however, requires effort. In a world rampant with negative influences, it is not easy to continue to live in a truly human manner. It is actually impossible without consistent effort to improve oneself. Moving up from the lower four of the Ten Worlds, the world of human beings is the first in which improving one's condition becomes a possibility.

Furthermore, those in the world of humanity, while vulnerable to negative influences, are also capable of exerting themselves in Buddhist practice and thereby advancing to the four noble worlds.

The World of Heavenly Beings

The name of this world derives from the Indic word *devaloka*, which means the place where gods and superhuman godlike beings reside.

In Buddhist philosophy, the world of heavenly beings, or heaven, refers to a condition of life in which one experiences the joy of having one's desires fulfilled. Hence, Nichiren says, "Joy is [the world] of heaven" ("The Object of Devotion for Observing the Mind," WND-1, 358).

Human beings experience many kinds of desire. There are fundamental or instinctual desires, such as for sleep and food. There are desires for material things, as well as social, intellectual and spiritual desires. In general, we can think of the world of heaven as the condition of joy that pervades our lives at having any of these various desires fulfilled.

But the joy associated with the world of heaven is not lasting; it eventually weakens and disappears. The world of heaven, therefore, is not the condition of genuine happiness that Buddhism aims to achieve.

From the Six Paths to the Four Noble Worlds

The six worlds discussed above, together referred to as the six paths, describe states of life easily influenced by external circumstances. Those who remain in them cannot enjoy true freedom or independence.

The aim of Buddhist practice is to transcend these six paths and build a self-determined happiness that is uncontrolled by the environment. The conditions of life a person develops through Buddhist practice are known as the four noble worlds, the worlds of voice-hearers (learning), cause-awakened ones (realization), bodhisattvas and Buddhas.

The World of Voice-Hearers and Cause-Awakened Ones

In Hinayana teachings, the two worlds of voice-hearers and cause-awakened ones (also called the worlds of learning and realization) represented the two highest states Buddhist practitioners could attain and are together called the "two vehicles."

"Voice-hearers" originally meant those who had achieved a partial awakening through hearing (listening to) the Buddha's teachings. In contrast, cause-awakened ones were those who had achieved an awakening on their own, through their connection with or observation of various phenomena.

The partial enlightenment that characterizes both worlds of the two vehicles consists of an awakening to the transience or impermanence of all things. Impermanence indicates the reality that all phenomena change with the passage of time and eventually die out and cease to exist. Those who possess the life condition of the two vehicles, having overcome the tendency to be attached to impermanent things, can view themselves and the world objectively, awakened to the truth that everything in this real world changes and perishes with the passage of time.

Nichiren Daishonin says: "The fact that all things in this world are transient is perfectly clear to us. Is this not because the worlds of the two vehicles are present in the human world?" ("The Object of Devotion for Observing the Mind," WND-1, 358). He is saying that within the world of humanity exists the potential for the life states of the two vehicles.

Considering the Ten Worlds as potential conditions of human life, we could say that the worlds of learning and realization represent states of awakening and self-determination that transcend those of the six paths. People in these states may be inquisitive, intellectual and creative. The shortcomings those in these conditions face, however, are complacency—the assumption that one has reached a pinnacle of development—and a preoccupation with personal attainment to the exclusion of concern and effort for the good of others. It is this tendency toward self-centeredness on the part of people of the two vehicles that caused early Mahayana Buddhist scriptures to deny them the possibility of attaining enlightenment.

The World of Bodhisattvas

Bodhisattvas are beings who relentlessly exert themselves to gain the enlightenment of a Buddha. Persons of the two vehicles, though regarding the Buddha as their teacher, do not believe themselves capable of attaining the same state of enlightenment as the Buddha. In contrast, bodhisattvas not only regard the Buddha as their teacher but also aim to realize the same supreme enlightenment. In addition, bodhisattvas believe that all people can attain Buddhahood and work to spread the Buddha's teaching widely to relieve people's suffering and lead them to happiness.

What distinguishes bodhisattvas is their strong spirit to seek the world of Buddhahood, the highest state a human being can manifest, as well as their efforts to share with others the benefits they have obtained through Buddhist practice. Bodhisattvas are filled, before all else, with a strong wish for people's happiness.

The world of bodhisattvas is a state of life in which one acts with a sense of mission for the sake of people and for the Law. Compassion is fundamental to this world. The Sanskrit term for compassion, *karuna* (Jpn *jihi*), is sometimes translated as "loving kindness" or "mercy." Regarding this, Nichiren Daishonin says: "Even a heartless villain loves his wife and children. He too has a portion of the bodhisattva world within him" ("The Object of Devotion for Observing the Mind," WND-1, 358). Here, Nichiren reminds us that all people, even the cruel and corrupt, have the potential for compassion.

It is the nature of those who exhibit the world of bodhisattvas to base their lives and actions upon compassion for all people.

The World of Buddhas

The world of Buddhas, or Buddhahood, is a supremely noble and virtuous state of life. The Sanskrit word *buddha* means "one who has awakened." A Buddha is someone enlightened to the Mystic Law, the wonderful law or principle that is the basis of all life and phenomena in the universe.

Specifically, "the Buddha" refers to Shakyamuni, also known as Gautama or Siddhartha, who lived and taught in India roughly 2,500 years ago.

The Buddhist sutras describe various other Buddhas such as Amida and Mahavairochana, but these are mythical figures intended to represent the wonder and greatness of a particular virtue or quality of the Buddha's enlightened state of life.

Nichiren Daishonin appeared in the Latter Day of the Law, the age in which Shakyamuni's teachings had been predicted to fall into decline and become ineffective in leading people to enlightenment. To save all people in the Latter Day from suffering, Nichiren manifested the world of Buddhahood in his own life as proof that an ordinary human being can do so. Because he established the way by which all people can attain Buddhahood, he is respected as the true Buddha of the Latter Day of the Law.

The world of Buddhahood is a life condition rich in noble virtue and good fortune. It emerges when individuals awaken to the reality that the source and foundation of their very lives is the Mystic Law. A Buddha is someone who opens this state of life within and thus embodies unsurpassed compassion and wisdom. And, fueled by that compassion and wisdom, a Buddha works constantly to enable all people to manifest the same world of Buddhahood.

All of us inherently possess the world of Buddhahood, but bringing that condition forth amid the reality of our lives is no easy matter. For that reason, the Daishonin inscribed the Gohonzon, the object of devotion, as an embodiment of the world of Buddhahood he had attained. He did this to provide a means for all to bring forth Buddhahood in their own lives.

The world of Buddhahood, the state that Nichiren manifested, in essence, is the law of Nam-myoho-renge-kyo. When we believe in the Gohonzon and strive to chant for our own happiness and that of others, we can tap the world of Buddhahood inherent within us and embody it in our lives.

In "The Object of Devotion for Observing the Mind," Nichiren refers to the deep connection between faith and our innate Buddhahood. He writes, "That ordinary people born in the latter age can believe in the Lotus Sutra is due to the fact that the world of Buddhahood is present in the human world" (WND-1, 358).

The Lotus Sutra reveals that all people are innately Buddhas; we human beings can believe in that teaching precisely because our lives fundamentally possess the world of Buddhahood.

Based on Nichiren's statement above, Nichikan, the great scholar of Nichiren Buddhism, writes, "A heart that strongly believes in the

Lotus Sutra is [another] name for the world of Buddhahood." The Lotus Sutra here means the Gohonzon. And the world of Buddhahood is none other than absolute happiness gained from basing one's life on chanting Nam-myoho-renge-kyo to the Gohonzon whatever our circumstances.

Buddhist texts, including Nichiren's writings, often liken the world of Buddhahood to a lion king. Like the lion king, those who have activated their Buddhahood neither fear nor are daunted by anything or anyone. It is a condition of courage, genuine peace, absolute happiness and enlightenment.

Adapted from an article in the October 2007 Daibyakurenge,
the Soka Gakkai's monthly study journal

Attaining Buddhahood in This Lifetime

The purpose of Buddhist faith and practice is to achieve the life state of a Buddha. By chanting Nam-myoho-renge-kyo to the Gohonzon with faith and striving to carry out practice for oneself and for others, anyone can achieve the state of Buddhahood or enlightenment in this lifetime. Nichiren Buddhism calls this important principle "attaining Buddhahood in this lifetime." It contrasts with the general belief in Buddhism, set forth in sutras other than the Lotus Sutra, that becoming a Buddha requires countless lifetimes of difficult practices.

Nichiren Daishonin says: "If votaries of the Lotus Sutra carry out religious practice as the sutra directs, then every one of them without exception will surely attain Buddhahood within his or her present lifetime. To cite an analogy, if one plants the fields in spring and summer, then, whether it be early or late, one is certain to reap a harvest within the year" ("The Doctrine of Three Thousand Realms," *The Writings of Nichiren Daishonin*, vol. 2, p. 88).

Some may wonder, *What does this have to do with me?* Most of us in the West, after all, have never given a thought to becoming a Buddha or attaining Buddhahood. Buddha, however, means "awakened one" and describes a condition of inexhaustible wisdom, life force, courage and compassion. In that respect, we could say becoming a Buddha simply means becoming a person who exhibits these qualities, a person who is deeply happy and fulfilled.

Attaining Buddhahood does not mean becoming something special or different from what we are. Nor does it refer to a transcendent state or entry after death into some pure realm removed from this world.

Regarding attaining Buddhahood, Nichiren says: "'Attain' means to open or reveal. It is to reveal that the beings of the Dharma-realm are Buddhas eternally endowed with the three bodies.[1] 'Buddhahood' means being enlightened to this" (*The Record of the Orally Transmitted Teachings*, p. 126). So, attaining Buddhahood means opening and revealing the Buddha nature that we already possess. We need not go somewhere special to do this. It is within the realities of daily living that we build a life condition of absolute happiness, which cannot be upset or destroyed by external circumstances.

Nichiren states, "Each thing—the cherry, the plum, the peach, the damson—in its own entity, without undergoing any change, possesses the eternally endowed three bodies" (OTT, 200). As this passage suggests, attaining Buddhahood means giving free and full play to our unique inherent qualities and leading a dynamic and most fulfilling way of life. The term eternally endowed in the above passage can also be translated as "uncreated." This means that a true Buddha is someone naturally endowed with all the qualities of a Buddha, and who displays these qualities just as he or she is, without any pretention or embellishment. To attain Buddhahood also means not only to remain unswayed by difficulties or hardships but also to use them as fuel for purifying and strengthening one's life.

Buddhahood is not a goal that we arrive at some point along the way. Rather, it means to devote ourselves to overcoming negative tendencies or influences and creating good based on the Mystic Law; it means to wage a continued struggle for the happiness of people. One who genuinely engages in this ongoing challenge can reveal the life condition of a Buddha. SGI members who fight tirelessly for kosen-rufu, therefore, can rightly be called Buddhas.

Relative Happiness and Absolute Happiness

Second Soka Gakkai president Josei Toda taught that there are two kinds of happiness: relative happiness and absolute happiness.

Relative happiness speaks of a condition in which one's material desires or immediate personal wishes are satisfied. While there is no limit to what we can hope or wish for, there is always a limit to what we can have materially and how long we can hold on to it. For example, we may get something we want at this moment, but the fulfillment we enjoy from getting it will not last. Through effort and planning, we may develop and adjust our circumstances to our liking, thinking this is happiness. But should those circumstances change or disappear, so will our happiness. Such happiness is called relative because it exists only in relation to external factors.

In contrast, absolute happiness means that living itself is happiness; being alive is a joy, no matter where we are or what our circumstances. It describes a life condition in which happiness wells forth from within. It is called absolute because it is not influenced by external conditions. Attaining Buddhahood means developing absolute happiness.

Beyond the troubles of just getting by in life, we often face unexpected problems. Happiness does not depend on whether or not we have problems, but how we perceive and deal with them. To cite an analogy, a person of little strength and experience who encounters a steep mountain path will view it as a daunting obstacle. But a strong, experienced hiker can confidently ascend a steep trail even while carrying a heavy backpack, enjoying the view along the way. In a similar way, one who has firmly established a life condition of absolute happiness can confidently face any difficulty. Problems can even become an impetus to bring forth a powerful life force, enabling one to calmly and confidently overcome any challenge.

For a strong mountain climber, the steeper and more rugged the mountain, the greater the enjoyment. Likewise, a person who has developed the wisdom and life force to overcome hardship will find society, which is rife with problems, to be a place for the creation of value and fulfillment.

SGI President Ikeda states: "Ultimately, happiness rests on how we establish a solid sense of self or being . . . Happiness does not lie in outward appearances nor in vanity. It is a matter of what you feel inside; it is a deep resonance in our lives" (*My Dear Friends in America*, third edition, pp. 478–79). In addition, the things that constitute relative happiness, such as possessions, relationships or circumstances, all disappear upon death. Absolute happiness, however, which is the life condition of a Buddha, exists on the level of life that is eternal and transcends life and death. It is a benefit that we can carry with us lifetime after lifetime.

Adapted from an article in the October 2010 Daibyakurenge, *the Soka Gakkai's monthly study journal*

Notes

1. Three bodies: A concept set forth in Mahayana Buddhism to organize different views of the Buddha appearing in the sutras. The three bodies are: The Dharma body, the reward body and the manifested body. The Great Teacher T'ien-t'ai maintained that the three bodies are not separate entities but three integral aspects of a single Buddha. From this viewpoint, the Dharma body indicates the essential property of a Buddha, which is the truth or Law to which the Buddha is enlightened. The reward body indicates the wisdom, or the Buddha's spiritual property, that enables the Buddha to perceive the truth. The manifested body indicates compassionate actions, or the physical property of a Buddha used to carry out compassionate actions to lead people to enlightenment.

The Gohonzon

A famous passage from the writings of Nichiren Daishonin states, "I, Nichiren, have inscribed my life in sumi ink, so believe in the Gohonzon with your whole heart" ("Reply to Kyo'o," *The Writings of Nichiren Daishonin*, vol. 1, p. 412).

Honzon is a Japanese word meaning "object of fundamental respect or devotion." The prefix *go* means "worthy of honor." While Nam-myoho-renge-kyo is the ultimate law of the universe, the Gohonzon is its graphic expression. As we chant Nam-myoho-renge-kyo, focusing on the Gohonzon, we activate within us the power of this Law.

Every religion has an object of devotion. In many, it is a supreme being or god. The many schools of Buddhism have traditionally revered the Buddha and the Buddha's teachings. The concept of the Buddha and the content of the teachings, however, have differed from school to school.

For example, Shakyamuni Buddha was an ordinary human being who achieved a profound awakening and dedicated his life to freeing people from suffering and leading them to enlightenment. But after his passing, people came to worship him as they would a deity. They prayed to his statue or image in hope of winning his blessings.

Nichiren taught that people who view the Buddha or the Law as separate from themselves cannot realize their full potential. He said, "If you think the Law is outside yourself, you are embracing not the Mystic Law but an inferior teaching" ("On Attaining Buddhahood in This Lifetime," WND-1, 3).

A Clear Mirror of Life

In contrast to worshiping the Buddha or Law as externals, the Great Teacher T'ien-t'ai of China, basing his teaching on the Lotus Sutra, set forth a meditative discipline for attaining enlightenment. He called this "observing the mind." T'ien-t'ai's philosophy recognized the potential for Buddhahood in all people. But his practice was too difficult to carry out amid the challenges of daily life. Only those of superior ability, living in secluded circumstances, had a chance of attaining enlightenment.

Nichiren Daishonin established a teaching and practice to directly awaken the innate enlightened nature in any human being—the practice of chanting Nam-myoho-renge-kyo (see pp. 11–15). Enlightenment, more than just a state of mind, encompasses the totality of our mental, spiritual and physical being, as well as our behavior. Introspection alone, as in T'ien-t'ai's teachings, is inadequate for attaining enlightenment.

Nichiren inscribed the Gohonzon to serve as a mirror to reflect our innate enlightened nature and cause it to permeate every aspect of our lives. SGI President Ikeda states: "Mirrors reflect our outward form. The mirror of Buddhism, however, reveals the intangible aspect of our lives. Mirrors, which function by virtue of the laws of light and reflection, are a product of human wisdom. On the other hand, the Gohonzon, based on the law of the universe and life itself, is the culmination of the Buddha's wisdom and makes it possible for us to attain Buddhahood by providing us with a means of perceiving the true aspect of our life" (*My Dear Friends in America*, third edition, p. 94).

And just as we would not expect a mirror to apply our makeup, shave our beards or fix our hair, when we chant to the Gohonzon, we do not expect the scroll in our altars to fulfill our wishes. Rather, with faith in the power of the Mystic Law that the Gohonzon embodies, we chant to reveal the power of our own enlightened wisdom and vow to put it to use for the good of ourselves and others.

Nichiren, emphasizing the nature of the Gohonzon's power, writes: "Never seek this Gohonzon outside yourself. The Gohonzon exists only within the mortal flesh of us ordinary people who embrace the Lotus Sutra and chant Nam-myoho-renge-kyo" ("The Real Aspect of the Gohonzon," WND-1, 832).

An Expression of Nichiren's Winning State of Life

From childhood, Nichiren Daishonin ignited within himself a powerful determination to rid the world of misery and lead people to lasting happiness. With this vow, he thoroughly studied the sutras and identified chanting Nam-myoho-renge-kyo as the practice that embodies the essence of Shakyamuni's teachings. In the course of propagating this practice, Nichiren overcame numerous harsh persecutions, including attempts on his life.

After the failed attempt to execute him at Tatsunokuchi in 1271, Nichiren began to inscribe the Gohonzon and bestow it upon staunch believers. Regarding this, he said: "From that time, I felt pity for my followers because I had not yet revealed this true teaching to any of them. With this in mind, I secretly conveyed my teaching to my disciples from the province of Sado" ("Letter to Misawa," WND-1, 896).

Nichiren emerged victorious over the most powerful religious and secular oppression, and resolved to leave a physical expression of his winning state of life so all future disciples could bring forth that same life condition.

Writing to his samurai disciple Shijo Kingo, he stated: "In inscribing this Gohonzon for [your daughter's] protection, Nichiren was like the lion king. This is what the sutra means by 'the power [of the Buddhas] that has the lion's ferocity.' Believe in this mandala with all your heart. Nam-myoho-renge-kyo is like the roar of a lion. What sickness can therefore be an obstacle?" ("Reply to Kyo'o," WND-1, 412).

The Treasure Tower

"The Emergence of the Treasure Tower," the 11th chapter of the Lotus Sutra, describes a gigantic tower adorned with precious treasures emerging from beneath the earth and hovering in the air. Nichiren explains that this tower is a metaphor for the magnitude of the human potential—the grandeur of the Buddha nature within all people (see "On the Treasure Tower," WND-1, 299). Next, the sutra describes the Ceremony in the Air—a vast assembly of Buddhas, bodhisattvas and beings of every description, gathering from all corners of the cosmos. The Buddha employs special powers to raise the entire assembly into the air before the treasure tower. He then begins preaching his teaching.

Nichiren chose to depict on the Gohonzon, in written form, key elements of this Ceremony in the Air. Nam-myoho-renge-kyo, representing the treasure tower, is inscribed down the center of the Gohonzon. Rather than a painted or sculpted image, which could not sufficiently capture the totality of a Buddha, Nichiren employed written characters on the Gohonzon to communicate the state of oneness with the Mystic Law that he realized in his own life. According to President Ikeda: "Such [a statue or image] could never fully express Nam-myoho-renge-kyo, the fundamental Law that includes all causes (practices) and effects (virtues). The invisible attribute of the heart or mind, however, can be expressed in words" (June 2003 *Living Buddhism*, p. 34).

President Ikeda also emphasizes: "Through our daily practice of reciting the sutra and chanting Nam-myoho-renge-kyo, we can join the eternal Ceremony in the Air here and now. We can cause the treasure tower to shine within us and to shine within our daily activities and lives. That is the wonder of the Gohonzon. A magnificent cosmos of life opens to us, and reality becomes a world of value creation" (June 2003 *Living Buddhism*, p. 32).

The Gohonzon Exists in Faith

While most can agree that everyone possesses a wonderful potential within, truly believing this about all people and living based on this belief is not easy. Nichiren Daishonin inscribed the Gohonzon so that anyone can believe in and activate his or her Buddha nature. Just having the Gohonzon, however, will not ensure this. Both faith and practice are essential to unlocking our powerful Buddha nature. Nichiren says: "This Gohonzon also is found only in the two characters for faith. This is what the sutra means when it states that one can 'gain entrance through faith alone' . . . What is most important is that, by chanting Nam-myoho-renge-kyo alone, you can attain Buddhahood. It will no doubt depend on the strength of your faith. To have faith is the basis of Buddhism" ("The Real Aspect of the Gohonzon," WND-1, 832).

The Banner of Propagation

Nichiren Daishonin also says, "I was the first to reveal as the banner of propagation of the Lotus Sutra this great mandala" ("The Real Aspect of the Gohonzon," WND-1, 831).

Today, the SGI, through the leadership of its three founding presidents—Tsunesaburo Makiguchi, Josei Toda and Daisaku Ikeda—has embraced the Gohonzon as Nichiren truly intended—as a "banner of propagation" of the Buddhist teaching that can lead humankind to peace and happiness. For that reason, members who chant Nam-myoho-renge-kyo to the Gohonzon and exert themselves in SGI activities to spread the Law in the spirit of the three presidents achieve remarkable growth, benefit and victory in their lives.

Faith Equals Daily Life

The purpose of religion should be to enable people to lead happy, fulfilling lives. Buddhism exists for this very reason. While many tend to view Buddhism as a reclusive practice of contemplation aimed at freeing the mind from the concerns of this world, this is by no means its original intent. Seeking to deny or escape the realities of life or society does not accord with the genuine spirit of Buddhism. Enlightenment, which Buddhism aims for, is not a transcendent or passive state, confined to the mind alone. It is an all-encompassing condition that includes an enduring sense of fulfillment and joy, and permeates every aspect of our lives, enabling us to live in the most valuable and contributive way. This idea is expressed in the SGI through the principle that "faith equals daily life."

Nichiren Daishonin stressed this idea from many angles in his writings, often quoting the Great Teacher T'ien-t'ai's statement that "no worldly affairs of life or work are ever contrary to the true reality" ("Reply to a Believer," *The Writings of Nichiren Daishonin*, vol. 1, p. 905). When, through our Buddhist practice, our inner condition becomes strong and healthy—when we bring forth the "true reality" of our innate Buddha nature—we can act with energy and wisdom to excel at school or work and contribute to the well-being of our families and communities.

Regarding the principle that faith equals daily life, "daily life" points to the outward expressions of our inner life. And "faith," our Buddhist practice, strengthens the power within us to transform our inner lives at the deepest level. When we apply our practice to the issues and problems we encounter in daily life, those challenges become stimuli—causes or conditions—that enable us to bring forth and manifest Buddhahood. Our daily lives become the stage upon which we carry out a drama of deep internal life reformation.

Nichiren writes: "When the skies are clear, the ground is illuminated. Similarly, when one knows the Lotus Sutra, one understands the meaning of all worldly affairs" ("The Object of Devotion for Observing the Mind," WND-1, 376). For us, "knowing the Lotus Sutra" means chanting Nam-myoho-renge-kyo courageously to the Gohonzon and participating in SGI activities for our own and others' happiness. This causes our Buddha nature to surge forth, infusing us with rich life force and wisdom. We in effect come to "understand the meaning of all worldly affairs." The teaching and practice of Buddhism enable us in this way to win in daily life.

A scholar recently noted that one reason the SGI has attracted such a diverse group of people over the years is that it emphasizes and encourages people to apply Buddhist practice to winning in their lives. This accords with Nichiren's emphasis on actual results as the most reliable gauge of the validity of a Buddhist teaching. As he says, "Nothing is more certain than actual proof" ("The Teaching, Practice, and Proof," WND-1, 478).

At monthly SGI discussion meetings, members share experiences that result from faith and practice, and joyfully refresh their determination to advance and grow. The Soka Gakkai's founding president, Tsunesaburo Makiguchi, established the discussion-meeting format before World War II. He described them as venues to "prove experimentally the life of major good" (*The Wisdom of the Lotus Sutra*, vol. 2, p. 118). Hearing and sharing experiences in faith give us insight into how Buddhist practice enriches people's lives and inspire us to strengthen our resolve. Discussion meetings are forums for confirming the purpose of Buddhism, which is to enable every person to win in life and become happy.

We should also understand that chanting Nam-myoho-renge-kyo produces the most meaningful rewards when accompanied by action or effort.

Any religion promising results without effort would be akin to magic. But even if we could get what we wanted through magic, we would not grow in character, develop strength or become happy in the process. Buddhist practice complements and strengthens the effects of any effort. A student may chant to ace a test, but the surest path to passing is to match such prayers with serious effort in study. The same applies to all matters of daily living.

The power of chanting Nam-myoho-renge-kyo to the Gohonzon is unlimited. It infuses us with the energy we need to keep striving and with the wisdom to take the best, most effective action. When we act wielding this energy and wisdom, we will undoubtedly see our prayers realized.

President Ikeda says: "The Gohonzon is the ultimate crystallization of human wisdom and the Buddha wisdom. That's why the power of the Buddha and the Law emerge in exact accord with the power of your faith and practice. If the power of your faith and practice equal a force of one hundred, then they will bring forth the power of the Buddha and the Law to the degree of one hundred. And if it is a force of ten thousand, then it will elicit that degree of corresponding power" (*Discussions on Youth*, second edition, p. 299).

Nichiren Daishonin instructed one of his disciples—a samurai named Shijo Kingo who lived in the military capital, Kamakura—as follows: "Live so that all the people of Kamakura will say in your praise that Nakatsukasa Saburo Saemon-no-jo [Shijo Kingo] is diligent in the service of his lord, in the service of Buddhism, and in his concern for other people" ("The Three Kinds of Treasure," WND-1, 851). At the time, Kingo had been subject to jealousy among his warrior colleagues, some of whom had spread rumors and made false reports about him to his feudal lord. But taking Nichiren's encouragement to heart, Kingo strove to act with sincerity and integrity, and thereby strengthened his ability to assist his lord—to do his job, in today's terms.

Nichiren also encouraged him that the entire significance or purpose of Buddhism lies in the Buddha's "behavior as a human being" (WND-1, 852) to fundamentally respect all people. This suggests that as Buddhists our sincere and thoughtful behavior toward others is of paramount importance.

Eventually Kingo regained his lord's trust and received additional lands, showing proof of the power of applying Nichiren's teaching to life's realities.

When President Ikeda visited the United States in 1990, he said to SGI-USA members: "I also sincerely hope that, treasuring your lives and doing your best at your jobs, each of you without exception will lead a victorious life. It is for this reason that we carry out our practice of faith" (*My Dear Friends in America*, third edition, p. 22).

We can view our immediate environment and responsibilities—at work, in our families and in our communities—as training grounds in faith and in life. In this way, we can use every difficulty as an opportunity to further activate our inherent Buddha nature through chanting Nam-myoho-renge-kyo, and win in the affairs of society. Then we can grasp the real joy of applying the principle that faith equals daily life.

Published in the May–June 2011 Living Buddhism, *pp. 17–19*

Changing Karma Into Mission

No one can avoid difficulties or problems. Buddhism encourages us to build happiness in the midst of reality, to grow, improve and become stronger while facing life's challenges. Nichiren Buddhism enables us to change every aspect of our lives for the better, permanently. The process called "changing karma" entails securing unwavering happiness by revolutionizing our lives at the very core. And seen from the Buddhist perspective of life and death, this happiness persists eternally, countless lifetimes into the future. Here we examine the principle of changing karma and the Buddhist practice for changing karma into mission.

What Is Karma?

Some of our problems and sufferings are caused by actions and decisions we have made in this life. But for some we can find no apparent cause. These may make us think, *I've done nothing wrong, so why is this happening to me?*

Buddhism teaches the principle of karma—that many events and conditions we experience in this lifetime result from actions we have made in previous lives. *Karma* is a Sanskrit word that means "action." It explains the workings of cause and effect that span the boundaries of life and death. Our actions of thought, speech and behavior are like seeds that become implanted in our lives. These causes can remain dormant as "latent effects" in the current and future lifetimes. At certain times under certain conditions, however, these reveal themselves as "manifest effects"—results, or karmic rewards, we experience in a tangible way. Karma, then, is the accumulation of actions from previous existences that remain dormant within us until they appear as effects in this lifetime. This karma can be either good or bad, though people tend to view "karma" as bad results stemming from bad actions in the past.

Buddhism teaches that life is not just a matter of the present, but a continuum of past, present and future lives—the "three existences" of life. Our actions at any moment become part of the continuum of cause and effect that spans these three existences. Bad causes in past lives or the present, such as disparaging or hurting others, stealing or lying and so on, express themselves in present or future lives as bad effects, bringing us suffering and problems. This is the principle of cause and effect that Buddhism and most Eastern philosophies generally teach. Nichiren Daishonin calls this the "general law of cause and effect." And while this principle is important to understand, being aware of it alone is not enough to change our lives.

Adopting this view would require that, in order to rid ourselves of bad karma, we negate every bad cause we have ever made by making a good cause in its place, one at a time, over countless lifetimes. Of course we would have to refrain from making any more bad causes as well. There would be no way to transform our sufferings arising from karma directly or quickly in this lifetime. Bound by this belief, many Buddhist sutras taught prior to the Lotus Sutra hold that changing one's karma requires countless eons of austere practices. This heavy view of karma ultimately inspires no hope.

Fortunately, Nichiren does not emphasize this general view of karma or cause and effect. Instead he focuses on the principle and practice of changing karma.

In "Letter from Sado," he makes a revolutionary pronouncement in stating, "My sufferings, however, are not ascribable to this causal law" (*The Writings of Nichiren Daishonin*, vol. 1, p. 305). Here, he expresses that the great persecutions he is facing cannot be explained by the general view of causality.

Rather, he continues, these sufferings arise from his slander of the Lotus Sutra in the present and past existences. By "Lotus Sutra" he does not simply mean a Buddhist scripture, but the deepest Law or principle the sutra embodies. This constitutes the correct teaching that all people can reveal their Buddhahood, the principle of respect for the value and dignity of the human being and the standard of striving for one's own happiness as well as the happiness of others. To slander the Lotus Sutra means to fail to recognize or to belittle these values intrinsic to life itself; it means to deny that one's life and the lives of all others are precious embodiments of the Mystic Law, which is the source of these ideals. This adverse relationship to the Mystic Law constitutes a deep-seated negative cause that gives rise to various forms of bad karma.

To change karma arising from rejecting or slandering this fundamental Law, we need to make the most fundamental good cause, which is to protect and spread that Law for the sake of people's happiness. This means to believe in the correct teaching of the Mystic Law, to practice it correctly, and to uphold, protect and teach it to many people. In this way, we can immediately change the direction of our lives, from one bound for suffering to one of increasing power and joy deriving from the law of life. This is the process of changing karma in Nichiren Buddhism. The source of this transformation is the practice of chanting Nam-myoho-renge-kyo. When we do so, "then the host of sins, like frost or dew, can be wiped out by the sun of wisdom" (*The Lotus Sutra and Its Opening and Closing Sutras*, p. 390). Referring to this passage from the Universal Worthy Sutra, Nichiren compares our past negative karma to frost or dew that has built up in one's life. When we believe in the Gohonzon and apply ourselves to chanting Nam-myoho-renge-kyo both for ourselves and for others, the world of Buddhahood emerges within our lives like the sun, dispelling our karmic impediments just as the warm morning sunlight evaporates frost or dew.[1]

Lessening Karmic Retribution

In the course of practicing Buddhism and working for kosen-rufu, we will inevitably face obstacles, negative influences and functions that attempt to block our way or interfere with our efforts.

Nichiren Daishonin taught that to encounter such opposition is in fact a benefit. That is because by meeting and winning over difficulties, we naturally carry out the process of "lessening our karmic retribution." The characters for the Japanese phrase *tenju kyoju*, often translated as "lessening one's karmic retribution," can literally be read "transforming the heavy and receiving it lightly." Left alone, the bad causes we have accumulated over many lifetimes reveal themselves as miserable results in this and future lifetimes. But through the benefit of devoting ourselves and leading others to the Mystic Law, the heavy consequences of our karma can quickly be lightened. That is, we can effectively rid ourselves of all our negative karma in this lifetime by experiencing its results in much lightened form as obstacles and troubles we challenge for the sake of kosen-rufu. For this reason, Nichiren Daishonin says that through the benefit of lessening karmic retribution, "The sufferings of hell will vanish instantly" ("Lessening One's Karmic Retribution," WND-1, 199). Difficulties, then, are important opportunities for ridding ourselves of bad karma and developing and strengthening ourselves.

Nichiren also says: "Iron, when heated in the flames and pounded, becomes a fine sword. Worthies and sages are tested by abuse. My present exile is not because of any secular crime. It is solely so that I may expiate in this lifetime my past grave offenses and be freed in the next from the three evil paths" ("Letter from Sado," WND-1, 303).

Voluntarily Assuming the Appropriate Karma

By persevering in faith despite hardships and thereby changing our karma, we find deeper meaning in living. In its "Teacher of the Law" chapter, the Lotus Sutra introduces the idea of "voluntarily assuming the appropriate karma."[2] It explains that bodhisattvas voluntarily give up the good karmic rewards due them as a result of their pure actions in past lives. Out of compassion, they choose instead to be born in an evil age so that they can teach people the principles of the Lotus Sutra and save them from suffering.

Such bodhisattvas experience suffering just as those who do so because of bad karma they formed in the past. Viewing ourselves as having made this choice—of voluntarily meeting and overcoming difficulties through faith out of compassion for others—gives us a new perspective on problems and suffering. We can see facing problems as something we do to fulfill our vow as a bodhisattva to save suffering people.

Only by dealing with hardships in life can we come to understand and empathize with people's suffering. With every problem we overcome through Buddhist faith and practice, we create a model for winning in life, a genuine experience through which we can encourage many others.

SGI President Ikeda expresses this process as "changing karma into mission" and explains: "We all have our own karma or destiny, but when we look it square in the face and grasp its true significance, then any hardship can serve to help us lead richer and more profound lives. Our actions in challenging our destiny become examples and inspirations for countless others.

"In other words, when we change our karma into mission, we transform our destiny from playing a negative role to a positive one. Those who change their karma into their mission have 'voluntarily assumed the appropriate karma.' Therefore, those who keep advancing, while regarding everything as part of their mission, proceed toward the goal of transforming their destiny" (August 2003 *Living Buddhism*, p. 50).

Adapted from an article in the October 2010 Daibyakurenge,
the Soka Gakkai's monthly study journal

Notes

1. For example, in "Letter to Niike," Nichiren writes: "Our worldly misdeeds and evil karma may have piled up as high as Mount Sumeru, but when we take faith in this sutra, they will vanish like frost or dew under the sun of the Lotus Sutra" (WND-1, 1026).

2. "Teacher of the Law," the 10th chapter of the Lotus Sutra, states, "Medicine King, you should understand that these people voluntarily relinquish the reward due them for their pure deeds and, in the time after I have passed into extinction, because they pity living beings, they are born in this evil world so they may broadly expound this sutra" (LSOC, 200).

Faith for Overcoming Obstacles

When we exercise with weights, the resistance strengthens our muscles and helps them grow. Similarly, the difficulties and challenges we encounter along the journey of life enable us to strengthen and improve our lives and our character. By applying our Buddhist practice to facing and winning over challenges, we train and develop our "muscles" of wisdom, life force, courage and compassion. These qualities accord with the state of life called Buddhahood, to which Buddhist practitioners aspire. When we view things this way, our problems become opportunities to build a solid foundation for unshakable happiness.

Buddhism describes two major categories of obstacles. The first is the "three obstacles and four devils"—obstacles encountered by those who strive to reveal and develop their Buddha nature. The second is the "three powerful enemies," which, the Lotus Sutra explains, attack genuine practitioners of the sutra who endeavor to spread its teachings. Since our Buddhist practice involves these two aspects, we need to be prepared to recognize and challenge both categories of obstacles.

The Three Obstacles and Four Devils

The "three obstacles and four devils" symbolize the internal and external functions that impede our progress toward genuine happiness, or enlightenment. Nichiren Daishonin quotes the Great Teacher T'ien-t'ai, who explained in *Great Concentration and Insight*: "As practice progresses and understanding grows, the three obstacles and four devils emerge in confusing form, vying with one another to interfere . . . One should be neither influenced nor frightened by them" (see "Letter to the Brothers," *The Writings of Nichiren Daishonin*, vol. 1, p. 501).

Here, Nichiren reiterates that these hindrances emerge "in confusing form," which means that their influence is usually not obvious or easy to recognize. We should be diligent in learning how to identify them and in developing the strength to win over them. Otherwise, we risk being "frightened" or "influenced" by these negative functions, allowing them to cloud our Buddha nature and obstruct our Buddhist practice.

The three obstacles are: (1) the obstacle of earthly desires; (2) the obstacle of karma (the negative actions or offenses we commit in this life); and (3) the obstacle of retribution (the negative effects of our actions in past lives, or karma). The four devils are: (1) the hindrance of the five components—hindrances caused by one's own physical and mental functions; (2) the hindrance of earthly desires—hindrances arising from greed, anger and foolishness; (3) the hindrance of death—one's own untimely death obstructing one's Buddhist practice or doubts arising from the untimely death of a fellow practitioner; and (4) the hindrance of the devil king of the sixth heaven—a strong negative influence taking various forms to cause practitioners to discard their Buddhist practice.

The three obstacles and four devils are functions that sap the bright, positive life condition we gain from our practice; they weaken our spirit to fight for our own happiness and that of others, leaving us with diminished courage and wisdom. In particular, the devil king of the sixth heaven is described as being most powerful.[1] It represents negative functions that can operate through influential people in our environment to discourage us from pursuing our Buddhist practice and keep us in a place of victimhood and suffering. The function arises from the human tendency to be ignorant of the fundamental dignity of life and to deny the noble potential for Buddhahood that all people possess. That tendency or ignorance is known as fundamental darkness. But more important than wondering what category of obstacle or devil our problems fall into is to recognize those things that hinder our Buddhist practice and challenge them with faith, prayer and action.

Lasting happiness can be achieved through learning to win over our inner darkness, or ignorance. SGI President Ikeda explains: "Buddhism is a struggle between the Buddha and the devil. It is by drawing out into the open, battling and defeating the three obstacles and four devils that we ourselves can become Buddhas" (January 2004 *Living Buddhism*, p. 48).

By continuously engaging in this challenge to activate our fundamental enlightenment, we can forge an indestructible foundation of happiness. When obstacles and devilish functions emerge, that is exactly the time to fight to change our karma and to win for the sake of our happiness.

As Nichiren writes, "The three obstacles and four devils will invariably appear, and the wise will rejoice while the foolish will retreat" ("The Three Obstacles and Four Devils," WND-1, 637). Urging us to never retreat, he calls on us to joyfully challenge and overcome our problems. The wise rejoice because they know that obstacles and opposition are the resistance that makes it possible for them to achieve enlightenment.

The Three Powerful Enemies

In "Encouraging Devotion," the 13th chapter of the Lotus Sutra, Shakyamuni describes three types of people who will persecute and try to stop the sutra's votaries from spreading its teachings (see *The Lotus Sutra and Its Opening and Closing Sutras*, pp. 232–34). These are: 1) arrogant lay people; (2) arrogant priests; and (3) arrogant false sages who conspire with secular authorities to persecute the sutra's votaries. The common thread among these "three powerful enemies" is arrogance—their belief that they are better than others.

The first of the powerful enemies is described as those ignorant of Buddhism who denounce and speak ill of those who practice the Lotus Sutra, who directly attack practitioners and try to ruin their societal standing or even their well-being.

The second of the powerful enemies comprises arrogant and cunning priests who, believing themselves superior to others, deviously try to ingratiate themselves with the powerful while looking down on the people. The enemies in this second category claim to have mastered Buddhism but refrain from practicing the correct Buddhist teaching. Instead, they slander and attack those who earnestly practice and uphold that teaching.

The third and most powerful enemy corresponds to priests who pretend to be and are revered as sages, but whose true motives are status and profit. Fearing a loss of prestige, they make false accusations to secular authorities and collude with those in power to persecute practitioners of the Lotus Sutra.

The sutra predicts that these three powerful enemies, intent on stopping the flow of kosen-rufu, will attack those who uphold, practice and spread the Lotus Sutra. Even if one can persevere under the attack of the first two, the last powerful enemy remains a formidable challenge because of the difficulty of perceiving the true identity of false sages.

Nichiren says: "A sword is useless in the hands of a coward. The mighty sword of the Lotus Sutra must be wielded by one courageous in faith" ("Reply to Kyo'o," WND-1, 412).

Encountering obstacles is part of life. No one can escape them. But rather than reacting out of fear, we practitioners of Nichiren Buddhism can instead summon courage as we wield the mighty sword of Nam-myoho-renge-kyo.

President Ikeda states: "Attaining Buddhahood in this lifetime entails a fierce struggle to change our karma, as well as to overcome the various challenges posed to our practice by the three obstacles and four devils, and the three powerful enemies. The trials of winter are unavoidable if we wish to soar into a brilliant springtime based on faith" (*Learning From the Writings: The Hope-filled Teachings of Nichiren Daishonin*, pp. 104–05).

By decisively facing and overcoming negative functions and obstacles, we can transform our karma and reveal our full potential while fulfilling our unique missions in life.

Adapted from an article in the October 2010 Daibyakurenge, *the Soka Gakkai's monthly study journal*

Notes

1. The devil king is said to rouse his ten forces, which are the various illusions that plague human beings. They are: (1) desire, (2) care and worry, (3) mental and physical hunger, (4) love of pleasure, (5) mental vagueness and lack of responsiveness, (6) fear, (7) doubt and regret, (8) anger, (9) preoccupation with wealth and fame, and (10) arrogance and contempt for others.

The Life of
Nichiren Daishonin

Nichiren Daishonin (1222–82) dedicated his life to propagating the Mystic Law—Nam-myoho-renge-kyo—motivated by an unwavering commitment and compassion to eradicate suffering and enable all people to reveal their innate Buddhahood. Hardship and persecution dogged him throughout his life as he sought to address and put an end to the evils obstructing people's happiness.

Early Years

Nichiren Daishonin[1] was born on February 16, 1222, in the coastal hamlet of Kataumi in Tojo Village of Nagasa District in Awa Province (part of present-day Kamogawa City in Chiba Prefecture). He was the son of commoners, his family earning its livelihood from fishing.

At the age of twelve, he began his schooling at a nearby temple called Seicho-ji. During this period, he made a vow to become the wisest person in Japan (see "The Tripitaka Master Shan-wu-wei," *The Writings of Nichiren Daishonin*, vol. 1, p. 175). He sought to gain the wisdom of the Buddhist teachings for overcoming the fundamental sufferings of life and death, and thereby lead his parents and all people to genuine happiness.

At the age of sixteen, in pursuit of a deeper understanding of the Buddhist teachings, he formally entered the priesthood at Seicho-ji, receiving instruction from Dozen-bo, a senior priest there. It was shortly thereafter, the Daishonin writes, that he attained "a jewel of wisdom as bright as the morning star" ("The Tripitaka Master Shan-wu-wei," WND-1, 176), which can be interpreted to mean wisdom regarding the Mystic Law that is the essence of Buddhism.

Nichiren then traveled to Kamakura, Kyoto, Nara and other centers of Buddhist learning, carefully studying the sutras and commentaries housed at leading temples such as Enryaku-ji on Mount Hiei, the headquarters of the Tendai school, and familiarizing himself with the core doctrines of each school. He confirmed that the Lotus Sutra is the foremost among all the Buddhist sutras and that the Law of Nam-myoho-renge-kyo to which he had awakened is the essence of the sutra and provides the means for freeing all people from suffering on the most fundamental level. He also awoke to his mission to spread Nam-myoho-renge-kyo as the teaching for people in the Latter Day of the Law to attain enlightenment.

[Note: *The Latter Day of the Law refers to the age when the teachings of Shakyamuni Buddha lose their power to lead people to enlightenment. It was generally regarded to mean the period two thousand years after the Buddha's passing. In Japan, it was believed that this age began in the year 1052.*]

The Declaration of the Establishment of His Teaching

Through his studies at leading Buddhist centers, Nichiren Daishonin confirmed his mission to spread the Mystic Law—Nam-myoho-renge-kyo—and the means by which to do so. He embarked on his struggle knowing that he would inevitably encounter great opposition and persecution.

On April 28, 1253, around noon at Seicho-ji, he refuted the Nembutsu and other Buddhist teachings of his day as erroneous and proclaimed Nam-myoho-renge-kyo to be the sole correct Buddhist teaching for leading all people in the Latter Day of the Law to enlightenment. This is known as the declaration of the establishment of his teaching. He was thirty-two years old. From around this time, he adopted the name Nichiren (literally, Sun Lotus).

Nichiren's denunciation of the Nembutsu doctrines on the occasion of declaring his teaching enraged Tojo Kagenobu, who was the local steward (an official of the Kamakura government who had the powers of law enforcement and tax collection) and an ardent Nembutsu believer. The latter planned an armed attack on the Daishonin, but the Daishonin narrowly managed to escape beforehand.

Nichiren then made his way to Kamakura, the seat of the military government. There, he took up residence in a small dwelling in Nagoe (at a site that later came to be known as Matsubagayatsu) and embarked in earnest on propagating his teaching. While refuting the error of the Nembutsu and Zen teachings, which had gained wide influence among the people of Kamakura, the Daishonin spread the teaching of Nam-myoho-renge-kyo.

It was during this early period of propagation that such well-known disciples as Toki Jonin, Shijo Kingo (Shijo Yorimoto) and Ikegami Munenaka converted to his teaching.

Submitting the Treatise "On Establishing the Correct Teaching for the Peace of the Land" and Encountering Persecution

In the period when Nichiren Daishonin began his propagation efforts in Kamakura, Japan had been experiencing a series of natural disasters and calamities, including extreme weather, severe earthquakes, famine, fires and epidemics. In particular, the devastating earthquake of the Shoka era, which struck the Kamakura region in August 1257, destroyed many homes and important buildings in Kamakura.

This disaster prompted the Daishonin to write the treatise "On Establishing the Correct Teaching for the Peace of the Land" (see WND-1, 6–26) to clarify the fundamental cause of people's suffering and set forth the means by which people could eradicate such suffering. On July 16, 1260, he submitted this treatise to Hojo Tokiyori, the retired regent of the Kamakura military government, who was still effectively the country's most powerful leader. It was the first time that Nichiren remonstrated with the authorities. This is known as his first remonstration with the government authorities.

In this treatise, he declared that the cause of the successive calamities lay with people's slander of the correct teaching of Buddhism and their reliance on erroneous doctrines. The most serious root cause, he asserted, was the Nembutsu teaching popularized in Japan by the priest Honen (1133–1212).

The Daishonin urged people to discontinue their reliance on such erroneous teachings and embrace faith in the correct teaching of Buddhism without delay, for this would ensure the realization of a peaceful and prosperous land. Continued reliance on erroneous teachings, he warned, would inevitably result in the country encountering internal strife and foreign invasion—the two calamities of the "three calamities and seven disasters" yet to occur.

[Note: The "three calamities and seven disasters" are described in various sutras, and differ slightly depending on the source. The three calamities include high grain prices or inflation (especially that caused by famine), warfare and pestilence. The seven disasters include natural disasters such as extraordinary changes of the stars and planets and unseasonable storms.]

However, the ruling authorities ignored Nichiren's sincere remonstration and, with their tacit approval, Nembutsu followers began plotting to persecute the Daishonin.

One evening shortly after Nichiren submitted his treatise "On Establishing the Correct Teaching for the Peace of the Land," a group of Nembutsu believers stormed his dwelling in an attempt to take his life. This is called the Matsubagayatsu Persecution. However, the Daishonin escaped unharmed. After this incident, he left Kamakura for a short period.

On May 12, 1261, the following year, having returned to Kamakura sometime earlier, Nichiren was arrested by the authorities and sentenced to exile in Ito of Izu Province. This is called the Izu Exile. After being pardoned from exile in February 1263, the Daishonin made his way back to Kamakura.

In 1264, he returned to his home province of Awa to visit his ailing mother. On November 11 of that year, Nichiren and a group of his followers were on their way to the residence of another follower named Kudo in Amatsu (also in Awa Province). At a place called Matsubara in Tojo Village, they were ambushed by a band of armed men under the command of the local steward, Tojo Kagenobu. In the attack, the Daishonin sustained an injury to his forehead and a broken left hand. One of his followers was killed at the site. This is called the Komatsubara Persecution.

The Tatsunokuchi Persecution and "Casting Off the Transient and Revealing the True"

In 1268, an official letter arrived in Kamakura from the Mongol empire demanding that Japan become one of its tributaries and threatening military attack should the demand be rejected. With this development, the danger of the calamity of foreign invasion befalling the nation became very real.

This spurred Nichiren Daishonin to write eleven letters of remonstration to top government officials, including the regent Hojo Tokimune, and the heads of major Buddhist temples in Kamakura.

In the letters, he stated that the impending danger of an invasion was just as he had predicted in his treatise "On Establishing the Correct Teaching for the Peace of the Land," and he expressed the hope that the priests of the various Buddhist schools would meet with him in an official public debate.

Neither the government leaders nor the religious establishment heeded the Daishonin's appeal. Rather, viewing Nichiren's community of believers as a threat to the existing power structure, the government began to take repressive measures against it.

Around this time, True Word priests were enjoying growing influence, the government having charged them with the mission of conducting prayers for the defeat of Mongol forces. Ryokan (Ninsho) of Gokuraku-ji (a temple in Kamakura), a priest of the True Word Precepts school, was also becoming more influential through his connections with powerful government figures.

The Daishonin fearlessly began to refute the errors of the established Buddhist schools that were exerting a negative influence on the people and society as a whole.

In the summer of 1271, in response to a prolonged drought, the government ordered Ryokan to pray for rain. Learning of this, Nichiren made a proposal to Ryokan: If Ryokan should succeed in producing rain within seven days, Nichiren would become his disciple; but if he failed to do so, then Ryokan should place his faith in the Lotus Sutra.

When his prayers failed to produce any rain after seven days had passed, Ryokan asked for a seven-day extension. Again no rain fell, but fierce gales arose instead. Ryokan had clearly lost the challenge.

Rather than honestly acknowledge defeat, however, Ryokan grew even more hostile toward the Daishonin. He contrived to bring accusations against Nichiren by filing a complaint with the government in the name of a Nembutsu priest who had close ties with him. He also used his influence with top government officials as well as their wives to have the Daishonin persecuted by the authorities.

Although Ryokan was widely respected among the populace as a devout and virtuous priest, he enjoyed the trappings of power and privilege, and colluded with government officials toward self-serving ends.

On September 10 of the same year (1271), Nichiren was summoned by the government and interrogated by Hei no Saemon-no-jo Yoritsuna (also known as Taira no Yoritsuna), the deputy chief of the Office of Military and Police Affairs (the chief being the regent himself). The Daishonin admonished him and emphasized the proper attitude for the nation's rulers based on the correct teaching of Buddhism.

Two days later, on September 12, Hei no Saemon-no-jo, leading a group of armed soldiers, conducted a raid on Nichiren's dwelling and arrested him, treating him as if he were a traitor. On that occasion, the Daishonin strongly remonstrated with Hei no Saemon-no-jo, warning that if he toppled him, "the pillar of Japan," the calamities of internal strife and foreign invasion would descend on the land. (The events on September 10 and 12 marked his second remonstration with the government authorities.)

Late that night, Nichiren was suddenly taken by armed soldiers to the beach at Tatsunokuchi, on the outskirts of Kamakura. This was at the directive of Hei no Saemon-no-jo and others who conspired to have the Daishonin secretly beheaded there. Just as the executioner raised his sword to strike, however, a brilliant orb of light burst forth from the direction of the nearby island of Enoshima, shooting northwest across the sky. The soldiers were terrified, and the attempt to kill the Daishonin had to be abandoned. This is called the Tatsunokuchi Persecution.

This persecution had extremely important significance for Nichiren. In triumphing over the Tatsunokuchi Persecution, he cast off his transient status as an ordinary, unenlightened person burdened with karma and suffering and, while remaining an ordinary human being, revealed his original, true identity as a Buddha possessing infinite wisdom and compassion (the Buddha of beginningless time or eternal Buddha). This is called "casting off the transient and revealing the true."[2]

Thereafter, the Daishonin's behavior was that of the Buddha of the Latter Day of the Law, and he went on to inscribe the Gohonzon for all people to revere and embrace as the fundamental object of devotion.

The Sado Exile

While the government was deliberating on his fate following the Tatsunokuchi Persecution, Nichiren Daishonin was detained for about a month at the residence of Homma Shigetsura (the deputy constable of Sado) in Echi, Sagami Province (part of present-day Atsugi City, Kanagawa Prefecture). During this period, the Daishonin's followers in Kamakura were subjected to many forms of persecution, including being unjustly accused of arson, murder and other crimes.

Eventually, Nichiren was sentenced to exile on Sado Island (part of present-day Niigata Prefecture). He departed from Echi on October 10, arriving at the graveyard of Tsukahara on Sado on November 1. The dwelling he was assigned there was a small, dilapidated shrine called the Sammai-do, which had been used for funerary rites. The conditions the Daishonin faced were truly harsh. It was bitterly cold on Sado, and he lacked sufficient food and warm clothing. In addition, he was surrounded by hostile Nembutsu followers who sought to take his life.

Nichiren's followers in Kamakura also continued to suffer persecution. Some were even imprisoned, banished or had their lands confiscated. The majority of his remaining followers began to have doubts and discarded their faith out of fear and a desire for self-preservation.

On January 16 and 17 the following year, 1272, several hundred Buddhist priests from Sado and nearby provinces on the mainland gathered at Tsukahara with the intent to kill the Daishonin. They were stopped by Homma Shigetsura, who proposed that they engage Nichiren in a religious debate instead. In the debate that ensued, the Daishonin thoroughly refuted the erroneous teachings of the various Buddhist schools of his day. This is known as the Tsukahara Debate.

In February, a faction of the ruling Hojo clan rose up in rebellion, and fighting broke out in Kamakura and Kyoto, the seat of the military government and the imperial capital, respectively. This is known as the February Disturbance or the Hojo Tokisuke Rebellion. The Daishonin's prediction of internal strife had come true just 150 days after declaring it in his remonstration with Hei no Saemon-no-jo at the time of the Tatsunokuchi Persecution.

In early summer of that year, the Daishonin was transferred from Tsukahara to Ichinosawa, also on Sado, but his life continued to be threatened by angry Nembutsu followers.

Nikko Shonin, who later became the Daishonin's successor, remained at his side throughout his Sado exile, faithfully following and serving him and sharing his sufferings. The Daishonin also steadily gained followers while on Sado Island, including Abutsu-bo and his wife, the lay nun Sennichi.

The Daishonin composed many important works during his exile on Sado. Of special significance are "The Opening of the Eyes" and "The Object of Devotion for Observing the Mind."

"The Opening of the Eyes," written in February 1272, explains that Nichiren Daishonin is the votary of the Lotus Sutra of the Latter Day of the Law, who is practicing in exact accord with the teachings of the Lotus Sutra. Ultimately, it reveals his identity as the Buddha of the Latter Day of the Law endowed with the three virtues of sovereign, teacher and parent to lead all people in the latter age to enlightenment. "The Opening of the Eyes" is referred to as "the writing clarifying the object of devotion in terms of the Person."

"The Object of Devotion for Observing the Mind," written in April 1273, presents the object of devotion of Nam-myoho-renge-kyo to be embraced by all people in the Latter Day of the Law in order to attain Buddhahood. It is referred to as "the writing clarifying the object of devotion in terms of the Law."

In February 1274, Nichiren was pardoned, and in March, he departed from Sado and returned to Kamakura.

Meeting Hei no Saemon-no-jo in April, the Daishonin strongly remonstrated with him, denouncing the government's actions in ordering priests to pray for the defeat of the Mongols based on the True Word and other erroneous Buddhist teachings. Further, responding to a direct question from Hei no Saemon-no-jo, he predicted that the Mongol invasion would most certainly take place before the year's end. This marked his third remonstration with the government authorities.

Just as Nichiren predicted, a large Mongol fleet attacked Kyushu, the southernmost of Japan's four main islands, in October 1274. This is referred to as the first Mongol invasion, with the second Mongol invasion occurring in May 1281.

With this event, the two predictions he had made in "On Establishing the Correct Teaching for the Peace of the Land"—those of internal strife and foreign invasion—had come true.

This was the third time that Nichiren had directly remonstrated with the government authorities and predicted that disasters would befall the country. Affirming that his predictions had been fulfilled, the Daishonin wrote, "Three times now I have gained distinction by having such knowledge" ("The Selection of the Time," WND-1, 579).

Taking Up Residence at Mount Minobu

When the government rejected his final remonstration, Nichiren Daishonin decided to leave Kamakura and take up residence in Hakii

Village on the slopes of Mount Minobu in Kai Province (present-day Yamanashi Prefecture). The local steward was Hakii Sanenaga, who had become a follower of the Daishonin through the propagation efforts of Nikko Shonin.

Nichiren moved to Mount Minobu in May 1274. His change of residence, however, was by no means a retreat from the world.

He composed many of his major works there, including "The Selection of the Time" and "On Repaying Debts of Gratitude." In these writings, he elucidated numerous important teachings—in particular, the Three Great Secret Laws (the object of devotion of the essential teaching, the sanctuary of the essential teaching and the daimoku of the essential teaching).

Through lectures on the Lotus Sutra, he devoted himself to fostering disciples who would carry out kosen-rufu in the future.

During this period, he also wrote many letters to his lay followers throughout the country, patiently instructing and encouraging them so they could persevere with strong faith, win in life and attain the state of Buddhahood.

The Atsuhara Persecution and the Purpose of the Daishonin's Appearance in This World

After Nichiren Daishonin moved to Mount Minobu, Nikko Shonin actively led propagation efforts in the Fuji District of Suruga Province (present-day central Shizuoka Prefecture), successfully convincing many Tendai priests and followers to abandon their old religious affiliations and begin practicing the Daishonin's teaching.

This prompted harassment and persecution by local Tendai temples, and threats were directed at those who had embraced Nichiren's teaching.

On September 21, 1279, twenty farmers, who were followers of Nichiren in Atsuhara, a village in Suruga Province, were arrested on trumped-up charges and taken to Kamakura. At the residence of Hei no Saemon-no-jo, they were subjected to harsh interrogation equivalent to torture. Though they were pressed to abandon their faith in the Lotus Sutra, they all remained true to their beliefs.

Three of the twenty followers arrested—the brothers Jinshiro, Yagoro and Yarokuro—were ultimately executed, while the remaining seventeen were banished from their places of residence. This series of events is known as the Atsuhara Persecution.

The example of these followers persevering in faith without begrudging their lives convinced Nichiren that humble, ordinary people without any position in society had developed sufficiently strong faith to withstand great persecutions. In "On Persecutions Befalling the Sage," dated October 1, 1279, in the twenty-seventh year after proclaiming his teaching, he refers to the purpose of his appearance in this world (see WND-1, 996).

While still little more than a child, Nichiren had vowed to become a person of wisdom who understood the essence of Buddhism and to free all people from suffering at the most fundamental level. The fulfillment of that vow was his life's guiding purpose. Expounding the teaching of Nam-myoho-renge-kyo, the fundamental Law for the enlightenment of all people, and revealing the Three Great Secret Laws—that is, the object of devotion of the essential teaching, the sanctuary of the essential teaching, and the daimoku of the essential teaching—he established the foundation for kosen-rufu that would endure for all time.

During the Atsuhara Persecution, ordinary people who embraced faith in Nam-myoho-renge-kyo that encompasses the Three Great Secret Laws dedicated themselves to kosen-rufu without begrudging their lives. Their appearance demonstrated that the Buddhism of Nichiren Daishonin was a teaching that would be championed by ordinary people, a teaching for the enlightenment of all humanity.

The Daishonin thus fulfilled the purpose of his appearance in this world.

At the time of the Atsuhara Persecution, Nichiren's followers strove in faith with the united spirit of "many in body, one in mind." His youthful disciple Nanjo Tokimitsu, steward of a village neighboring Atsuhara, worked tirelessly to protect his fellow believers.

The Daishonin's Death and Nikko Shonin's Succession

On September 8, 1282, Nichiren Daishonin, who was in declining health, left Minobu, where he had resided for nine years. He departed with the stated intent of visiting the therapeutic hot springs in Hitachi Province (part of present-day Ibaraki and Fukushima prefectures) at the recommendation of his disciples. When he arrived at the residence of his follower Ikegami Munenaka (the elder of the Ikegami brothers) in Ikegami in Musashi Province (present-day Ota Ward, Tokyo), he began to make arrangements for after his death.

On September 25, in spite of being gravely ill, he is said to have given a lecture to his followers on his treatise "On Establishing the Correct Teaching for the Peace of the Land."

Nichiren passed away at Ikegami Munenaka's residence on October 13, 1282, at the age of sixty-one, bringing to a close his noble life as the votary of the Lotus Sutra.

After Nichiren Daishonin's death, only Nikko Shonin carried on his mentor's fearless spirit and actions for kosen-rufu. Based on his awareness as Nichiren's successor, Nikko continued to speak out against slander of the Law and to remonstrate with the government authorities. He treasured every one of the Daishonin's writings, referring to them by the honorific name *Gosho* (honorable writings), and encouraged all disciples to read and study them as the sacred scripture for the Latter Day of the Law. He also fostered many outstanding disciples who exerted themselves in Buddhist practice and study.

Notes:

1. Nichiren Daishonin adopted the name Nichiren, which uses the Chinese characters for "sun" and "lotus," at the age of thirty-two, around the time he established his teaching of Nam-myoho-renge-kyo. For convenience, the name Nichiren is used throughout this article.

2. Casting off the transient and revealing the true: The revealing of a Buddha's true status as a Buddha, and the setting aside of that Buddha's provisional or transient identity. (See *The Soka Gakkai Dictionary of Buddhism*, pp. 71–72).

A Timeline of Nichiren Daishonin's Life

1222

February 16: Born in Kataumi, Tojo Village, Nagasa District, Awa Province (today, part of Chiba Prefecture)

(**Age 1**—at that time in Japan, as soon as a child was born, he or she was considered to be 1 year old)

1253

(**Age 32**)

April 28: Declares the establishment of his teaching at Seicho-ji, a temple in Awa Province

1260

(**Age 39**)

July 16: Submits "On Establishing the Correct Teaching for the Peace of the Land" to retired regent Hojo Tokiyori—his first official remonstration with the sovereign. Soon after, attacked by Nembutsu believers who tried to take his life (known as Matsubagayatsu Persecution).

1261

(**Age 40**)

May 12: Exiled to Izu Peninsula

1264

(**Age 43**)

November 11: Komatsubara Persecution

1268

(**Age 47**)

October 11: Sends eleven letters of remonstration to key figures in Kamakura

1271

(**Age 50**)

September 12: Tatsunokuchi Persecution. Thereafter begins inscribing the Gohonzon for his disciples

October 10: Sado Exile begins

1272	(Age 51)
	January 16–17: Tsukahara Debate
	February: Revolt breaks out in Kyoto and Kamakura; writes "The Opening of the Eyes"
1273	(Age 52)
	April 25: Writes "The Object of Devotion for Observing the Mind"
1274	(Age 53)
	March 26: Returns to Kamakura from Sado
	April 8: Meets Hei no Saemon; predicts Mongols will attack Japan within the year
	May 17: Takes up residence at Mount Minobu
	October: Mongol forces invade the southern island of Kyushu
1279	(Age 58)
	September 21: Twenty farmers arrested for their beliefs
1281	(Age 60)
	May: Mongols invade Kyushu a second time
1282	(Age 61)
	October 13: Dies at the residence of Ikegami Munenaka at Ikegami in Musashi Province

The History of the Soka Gakkai

(1) The Founders of the Soka Gakkai

The Soka Gakkai has its origins in the mentor-disciple relationship that existed between the organization's first president, Tsunesaburo Makiguchi, and its second president, Josei Toda.

Makiguchi was born on June 6, 1871, in a small port community on Japan's northwest coast, in what is today Kashiwazaki City, Niigata Prefecture. He spent much of his youth studying and working in Hokkaido, Japan's northernmost major island. At eighteen, he entered a teachers' training facility and, after graduating, became an elementary school teacher.

While a student, Makiguchi had developed a deep interest in geography. As a teacher, he continued to refine his ideas on the subject and on how best to teach it. In 1901, he left Hokkaido for Tokyo, and two years later published his first major work, *The Geography of Human Life*. In it, he rejects the traditional method of studying geography through rote memorization. He instead offers a systematic approach to education based on the relationship human life shares with nature and society.

Before becoming principal of Tosei Elementary School in 1913, Makiguchi worked a variety of jobs editing educational periodicals, teaching foreign students, developing textbooks and establishing correspondence courses for young women unable to receive a formal education.

On February 11, 1900, Josei Toda was born on Japan's central west coast in what today is Kaga City, Ishikawa Prefecture. Two years later, his family moved to the west coast of Hokkaido to Atsuta Village. After graduating from Atsuta Higher Elementary School (equivalent to middle school), he studied independently while working, eventually obtaining a provisional teaching license. In June 1918, Toda became an associate elementary school teacher.

Josei Toda Encounters His Mentor

Between 1913 and 1932, Makiguchi refined his educational theories and their practical applications while continuing his career as a principal. He advocated community studies in which students learn about and appreciate their communities. And he pursued ways to assure that disadvantaged children received equal opportunities in education, going beyond the classroom to care for his students. He bought lunches, for example, for students who couldn't afford their own and, on cold days, welcomed them with hot water to warm their hands.

In 1920, Toda visited Tokyo, where he was introduced to Makiguchi. The two discussed at length Japan's future as well as educational practice and research. A short while later, Toda moved to Tokyo and taught at Nishimachi Elementary, where Makiguchi was principal. Toda worked with and supported Makiguchi for the next twenty-three years.

The Value-Creating Education Society

Toda followed his mentor to Mikasa Elementary School. Then in 1923, when Makiguchi was transferred to his next school, Toda established Jishu Gakkan, a private preparatory school for students taking the competitive middle school examinations. Here, Makiguchi freely pursued his research and developed his educational theories.

When Makiguchi encountered Nichiren Buddhism, he saw that the teachings of Nichiren Daishonin resonated deeply with his ideals. In 1928, at fifty-seven, Makiguchi converted to Nichiren Buddhism. Toda followed suit.

Fully supporting Makiguchi's goal of publishing his educational theory, Toda edited and organized Makiguchi's years of notes on his educational research, practices and experience. Toda even invested his own funds to publish Makiguchi's work.

On November 18, 1930, with Toda's dedicated assistance, Makiguchi published the first of four volumes of *Soka kyoikugaku taikei* (The Sytem of Value-Creating Pedagogy). Tsunesaburo Makiguchi is listed as the author, Josei Toda, the publisher, and the publishing entity as "Soka Kyoiku Gakkai" (Value-Creating Education Society)—the predecessor of the Soka Gakkai (Value Creation Society). This publication date is also considered the day of the Soka Gakkai's founding.

Makiguchi in this work uses the word *soka*, which means value creation—a term derived from discussions between Toda and Makiguchi. Soka encompasses Makiguchi's long-developed theory that the purpose of education and of life is to create happiness, and in order to do that one must know how to create value. He writes: "We begin with the recognition that humans cannot create matter. We can, however, create value. Creating value is, in fact, our very humanity. When we praise persons for their 'strength of character,' we are really acknowledging their superior ability to create value."[1]

Practicing Nichiren Buddhism

In 1937, the Soka Kyoiku Gakkai began meeting regularly as an organization of educators who supported the theory of Soka education. But it quickly extended membership to noneducators and developed into an organization of people of diverse backgrounds and occupations. Their common interest lie in applying the teachings of Nichiren Buddhism to transforming their lives and Japanese society.

Eventually, the Soka Kyoiku Gakkai became a society of lay practitioners of the Nichiren Shoshu school. However, instead of depending on priests as other lay Buddhist organizations did, Makiguchi and Toda were fully responsible for running all meetings and giving guidance in faith. The Soka Gakkai was, from its inception, an organization of lay believers not restricted by the priesthood's formalities.

Since its establishment, the practice of Soka Gakkai members has been based on the original intent of Nichiren Daishonin and of Buddhism itself: helping people realize genuine happiness through practice and faith, and striving for the peace and prosperity of society. In the 1930s and early 1940s, the Soka Kyoiku Gakkai grew steadily. Through propagation efforts, discussion meetings in members' homes and occasional larger gatherings, it reached a membership of about three thousand households.

A Battle Against Militarism

By the mid-1930s, the Japanese government had begun placing restrictions on its citizens as a way to enforce support of its war effort. It aimed to strengthen public solidarity and nationalism by requiring citizens to uphold the state religion, Shinto, and its belief in the divinity of the Emperor and the nation. Makiguchi and Toda attracted official scrutiny by refusing to compromise the humane principles of Nichiren Buddhism and by pointing out the erroneous thinking, rooted in Shintoism, that was leading the country into war. The repressive Special Higher Police began to keep Soka Kyoiku Gakkai discussion meetings under surveillance.

By early 1940, religious organizations faced increasing pressure to uphold Shinto and incorporate it into their beliefs. In June 1943, Nichiren Shoshu priests, fearing government sanctions, accepted a Shinto talisman and instructed the Soka Kyoiku Gakkai leaders to direct its members to do the same.

The priests' actions directly contradicted the intent of Nichiren Daishonin and Nikko Shonin. Instead of courageously protecting the Buddhist Law, they compromised it in deference to the Shinto belief system invoked to promote war. In fact, the priesthood publicly praised Japan's declaration of war on the United States and Great Britain.

In contrast, despite mounting pressures, Makiguchi and Toda refused to accept the Shinto talisman and resolutely upheld Nichiren's spirit to protect the correct Buddhist teaching.

On July 6, 1943, Makiguchi was arrested while attending a discussion meeting in Izu. On the same day, Toda was arrested in Tokyo, along with twenty-one other Soka Kyoiku Gakkai leaders. They were charged with treason and violating the Peace Preservation Law, which targeted dissent against the government. Among those arrested, only Makiguchi and Toda refused to compromise their beliefs throughout the intense interrogations.

President Toda's Profound Awakening

In prison, Makiguchi continued to share Nichiren Buddhism even with his interrogators, pointing out the error of Japan's religious and war policies. Never submitting to their demands, he upheld his conviction in Nichiren Buddhism with his entire being.

Toda's greatest concern was for his elderly mentor. He prayed fervently: "I'm still young. My mentor is seventy-three. Please, if they'll release him even one day sooner, let me take the blame for both of us."[2]

From early 1944, Toda earnestly chanted Nam-myoho-renge-kyo in his jail cell, repeatedly reading the Lotus Sutra. He pondered the meaning of a passage that perplexed him in the Immeasurable Meanings Sutra—the prologue to the Lotus Sutra—that describes the essence of the Buddha with thirty-four negations. After deep prayer and contemplation, he came to the realization that the Buddha is essentially life itself; this life of the Buddha exists within himself and all people, as well as in the vast universe.

Then, in November, after chanting more determinedly than ever, he awakened to the truth that he himself was among the Bodhisattvas of the Earth. In the Lotus Sutra, these are the bodhisattvas entrusted with the mission to spread the sutra's teaching in the Latter Day of the Law, the impure age after Shakyamuni Buddha's passing that corresponds with the present.

On November 18, 1944, Makiguchi died of malnutrition in the Tokyo Detention House at age seventy-three. His death coincides with the anniversary of the Soka Kyoiku Gakkai's founding. Undeterred until the end, he lived in accord with Nichiren's teachings, dedicated to restoring the Daishonin's spirit to save all people from suffering by spreading Nam-myoho-renge-kyo.

His disciple, Toda, through the enlightenment he experienced in prison, awakened to his mission as a leader of kosen-rufu. This profound awakening became the starting point for the Soka Gakkai's development in the postwar era.

After the war, at Makiguchi's memorial in 1946, Toda expressed his gratitude to his mentor: "In your vast and boundless compassion, you let me accompany you even to prison. As a result, I could read with my entire being the passage from the Lotus Sutra 'those persons who had heard the Law dwelled here and there in various Buddha lands, constantly reborn in company with their teachers.'[3] The benefit of this was coming to know the essential purpose of a Bodhisattva of the Earth, and to absorb with my very life even a small degree of the sutra's meaning. Could there be any greater happiness than this?"[4]

The passage "those persons . . . reborn in company with their teachers" signifies the deep bond between mentor and disciple who always strive together for the happiness of humanity. Josei Toda's words express his deep sense of gratitude toward his mentor, Tsunesaburo Makiguchi.

(2) The Development of the Soka Gakkai in Postwar Japan

Josei Toda was released from prison on July 3, 1945. Though physically frail, he burned with a fierce resolve to rebuild the Soka Kyoiku Gakkai, which had virtually dissolved during World War II. From early 1946, Toda began lecturing on the Lotus Sutra and resumed discussion meetings and propagation efforts. He renamed the organization the Soka Gakkai (Value Creation Society), dropping the word *kyoiku*, meaning "education" or "pedagogy," reflecting a broader commitment to the peace, happiness and prosperity of society.

Daisaku Ikeda's Early Years

Daisaku Ikeda was born on January 2, 1928, in Ota Ward, Tokyo. Beginning in 1937, his four older brothers were drafted into Japan's military, which was waging a war of aggression in China. He was thirteen when the Pacific War broke out in 1941. Though struggling with tuberculosis, he supported his family by working at a munitions factory.

Ikeda was painfully aware of the tragedies of war. His family lost two homes in air raids. His eldest brother, Kiichi, on leave from the warfront, shared accounts of cruelty perpetrated by Japan's military that deeply saddened and angered Ikeda. When Kiichi died in battle, the pain deepened, compounded by his parents' grief.

When the war ended, Ikeda, in his late teens, sought meaning amid the pain and chaos of a devastated Japan. The values esteemed during wartime had proven to be fraudulent; like many youth his age, he was tormented by a spiritual void.

Ikeda attended his first Soka Gakkai discussion meeting on August 14, 1947. When introduced to Toda, Ikeda posed questions about life, patriotism, the emperor and the meaning of Nam-myoho-renge-kyo. Toda's answers were to the point, logical and without pretense, expressing a powerful conviction. *How succinctly he answers!* Ikeda thought. *There is no confusion in him. I think I can believe and follow this man.*[5]

Ikeda respected the fact that Toda had been imprisoned for his refusal to compromise his convictions in the face of pressure from Japan's militarist government. As their dialogue concluded, Ikeda asked if he could study under Toda.[6]

Ten days later, on August 24, he joined the Soka Gakkai, vowing to regard Toda as his mentor. In January 1949, two years after beginning his Buddhist practice, he was hired at Toda's publishing company as the editor of a youth magazine.

Daisaku Ikeda Fully Supports His Mentor

In July 1949, the Soka Gakkai launched its Buddhist study magazine, *Daibyakurenge*. Later that year, the postwar economy worsened and the publishing company foundered. The youth magazine Ikeda had been editing was suspended. He quickly switched gears to devote himself fully to building up Toda's new credit association, which soon faced severe setbacks. He gave everything to support his mentor in business and in private matters, as well as in his responsibility to lead the Soka Gakkai.

In 1950, economic disorder intensified, seriously impairing Toda's entrepreneurial efforts. Though Toda's businesses had financed the initial growth of the Soka Gakkai, as his enterprises faltered and his debt grew, some members—especially those connected to his unsuccessful credit association—lost confidence in him and the Soka Gakkai. On August 23, the credit association was suspended. To avoid burdening the organization with his financial struggles, Toda resigned as general director of the Soka Gakkai on August 24.

One by one, Toda's employees left, but he remained steadfast, devoting his entire being to repaying the company's massive debt. Ikeda fervently supported him, determined to help Toda become financially solvent and to see him become president of the Soka Gakkai. Toda began privately tutoring his young disciple, who a year earlier had quit night school to fully support his mentor, in a variety of academic subjects and in Buddhism.

Toda shared his vision for the future with Ikeda. His goals ranged from starting a newspaper for the Soka Gakkai to founding a university. In time, both the newspaper *Seikyo Shimbun* (1951) and Soka University (1971) emerged as the fruit of their joint efforts.

Josei Toda Becomes Second President of the Soka Gakkai

Josei Toda and Daisaku Ikeda struggled intensely between 1950 and 1951 to turn Toda's financial situation around. Toda resolved: "Whatever hardship may befall me, I must put it aside. This I will not do for my own sake but for the cause of fulfilling my mission.

I must not by any means leave even a single teaching of Nichiren Daishonin's unfulfilled."[7]

During this tumultuous time, Ikeda strove to fulfill his deepest wish—that his mentor be freed from his constricting financial situation and become president of the Soka Gakkai.

Within a year, Toda's financial difficulties were behind him, though he and Ikeda suffered from ongoing health troubles. Ikeda describes the struggles of that period as "the deciding factors of the Soka Gakkai's development and existence today."[8]

On May 3, 1951, Josei Toda became the second Soka Gakkai president. In his inaugural address, he vowed to accomplish a membership of 750,000 households. At the time, active Soka Gakkai families numbered approximately three thousand. Many in attendance could not comprehend how his goal would be achieved. Toda, however, had already begun preparations for a widespread propagation movement and was so confident that he told the members, "If my goal should not be attained by the end of my life, you need not hold a funeral for me, but just throw my remains into the sea off Shinagawa, all right?"[9]

Just prior to becoming president, on April 20, Toda launched the Soka Gakkai's newspaper, *Seikyo Shimbun*. He formed the women's division on June 10, the young men's division on July 11 and the young women's division on July 19.

In January 1952, Toda assigned Ikeda responsibility for the organization's Kamata Chapter. Ikeda devoted himself to meeting personally with and encouraging many members, and the following month, the chapter's membership increased by an unprecedented 201 households.

Toda firmly believed that diligent and correct study of Nichiren's writings was indispensable for the progress of kosen-rufu. He commissioned former high priest and Nichiren Buddhist scholar Nichiko Hori to help compile all of Nichiren's existing writings.

Gosho zenshu (The Collected Writings of Nichiren Daishonin) was published in April 1952, marking the 700th anniversary of the establishment of Nichiren's teachings. This made it possible for Soka Gakkai members to make the writings and teachings of Nichiren Daishonin a solid foundation for their Buddhist practice. In September, the Japanese government formally recognized the Soka Gakkai as a religious organization.

Ikeda, in the meantime, took on various organizational responsibilities. In January 1953, he became leader of the young men's division First Corps, and in April, he was appointed acting Bunkyo Chapter leader. The following March, he became the Soka Gakkai youth division leader.

Struggles With Authority

Nichiren Daishonin's determination to establish "the correct teaching for the peace of the land" defined his lifelong battle for the happiness of all people and realizing peace in society. Based on that same spirit, and to confront corruption in politics that caused people suffering and had led to religious repression, the Soka Gakkai for the first time endorsed candidates for the national parliament in April 1955.

Daisaku Ikeda led propagation efforts in the Kansai region, which resulted in Osaka Chapter growing by an unprecedented 11,111 households in the single month of May 1956. In July, Ikeda was put in charge of the Soka Gakkai election effort in Osaka.

Three candidates sponsored by the organization in Osaka won seats in the national elections. With this victory, the Soka Gakkai came to be regarded as an influential popular movement. At the same time, it faced heightened opposition from various groups that felt threatened by its success. For example, in June 1957, Ikeda went to Hokkaido, where the Yubari branch of the Japan Coal Miners Union, which had strong links to the country's Communist Party, had attempted to oppress and intimidate local coal miners who belonged to the Soka Gakkai. He protested such treatment, taking action through debate and dialogue to resolve the problem.

Immediately after this, on July 3, 1957, the Osaka police arrested and detained Ikeda, falsely charging him with election fraud, though other Soka Gakkai members had naively committed the infractions.

Ikeda was interrogated for fifteen days. Prosecutors threatened to arrest Toda if Ikeda did not confess to the charges. Toda's health was failing, and Ikeda could not bear the thought of his mentor returning to jail. To protect his mentor, Ikeda conceded. On July 17, he was indicted and released from the Osaka Detention Center. After a trial that continued for four years, he was found innocent of all charges on January 25, 1962.

Entrusting the Future of Kosen-rufu to the Youth

On September 8, 1957, Josei Toda passionately and publicly condemned all use of nuclear weapons, calling for their immediate abolition. Because of the mass death and devastation brought about by nuclear weapons, Toda denounced those who would use them as "devils" and "evil incarnate." He vowed to defeat the dark tendency in human life that would justify their use. This declaration set the tone for the Soka Gakkai's future peace movement.[10]

In December, the organization's membership reached 750,000 households—Toda's ultimate goal. In March 1958, the Grand Lecture Hall, donated by the Soka Gakkai, was completed at the head temple, Taiseki-ji, near Mount Fuji.

On March 16, six thousand youth assembled from throughout Japan at Taiseki-ji. At this gathering, though weakened by illness, Toda boldly passed the responsibility for accomplishing kosen-rufu to the youth, declaring, "The Soka Gakkai is the king of the religious world."[11] March 16 is celebrated today as Kosen-rufu Day.

On April 2, Toda died at age fifty-eight. Having drawn upon his enlightenment in prison as a source of strength, he had succeeded in rebuilding the Soka Gakkai and creating a solid foundation for kosen-rufu. His legacy includes the numerous successors he raised, among them the future third president of the Soka Gakkai, his closest disciple, Daisaku Ikeda.

(3) Establishing a Worldwide Network of Buddhist Humanism

On May 3, 1960, Daisaku Ikeda was inaugurated third president of the Soka Gakkai. He declared, "Though I am young, from this day I will take leadership as a representative of President Toda's disciples and advance with you another step toward the substantive realization of kosen-rufu."[12]

Determined to fulfill second Soka Gakkai president Josei Toda's wish to spread Nichiren Buddhism worldwide, on October 2, 1960, five months after becoming president, he visited nine cities in North and South America. In each country he visited, President Ikeda encouraged the Soka Gakkai members living there, most of whom were Japanese immigrants.

In New York, President Ikeda and his party visited the United Nations headquarters. There, he contemplated the role and potential of that international body in creating peace in the world. He has continued since then to support the United Nations and offer, through proposals and dialogues, a vision of the vital role it can play as an agent representing the will of ordinary people around the world for peace and working toward that common aim. In 1983, President Ikeda wrote his first peace proposal to the United Nations, offering a

perspective and detailed suggestions on issues such as nuclear abolition, the environment and strengthening the United Nations. He has
submitted a peace proposal each year since.

In January 1961, his travels included a visit to India. During the
trip, and particularly at Bodh Gaya—the place where Shakyamuni
attained enlightenment—he pondered creating an institution dedicated to researching Asian philosophy and culture as a means to
promote dialogue and peace. The following year, he established the
Institute of Oriental Philosophy.

In 1963, he founded the Min-On Concert Association, dedicated
to fostering peace through cultural and artistic exchange. He writes:
"Cultured people value peace and lead others to a world of beauty,
hope and bright tomorrows. Tyrannical authority, on the other hand,
only leads people to darkness—the opposite of art.

"For that reason, nurturing and spreading an appreciation for art
and culture are crucial in creating peace."[13]

President Ikeda traveled extensively throughout Japan to
encourage Soka Gakkai members. He focused on raising the next
generation of leaders, conducting lectures on Nichiren Daishonin's
teachings for student division representatives. In June 1964, he
created the high school division and in 1965, the junior high school
and elementary school divisions.

In 1965, he began writing his serialized novel *The Human
Revolution*, which details President Toda's struggle to reconstruct
the Soka Gakkai after being released from prison at the end of World
War II. This and its ongoing sequel, *The New Human Revolution*,
chronicle the history of the Soka Gakkai spanning eighty years.

Forging Peace Through Dialogue

To create pathways to peace, President Ikeda often exchanges views
with cultural, political, educational and artistic leaders from around

the world—an estimated sixteen hundred such encounters thus far. President Ikeda's best known dialogue, with eminent British historian Arnold J. Toynbee, took place over two-and-a-half years in the early 1970s. Their discussion opened many doors for him to meet and exchange views with notable thinkers over the ensuing years, including former Soviet president Mikhail Gorbachev, Nobel Peace laureates Linus Pauling and Betty Williams, futurist Hazel Henderson and many others.

In 1974, when he visited China, President Ikeda saw people living in fear of Soviet attack. He soon after visited the Soviet Union to confirm with its leaders that it would not attack China. He returned to China to convey this assurance. In one year, President Ikeda engaged in intensive dialogues with political figures of these two countries to nurture bonds of trust and plant seeds of peace.

Leon Strijak of Moscow University interpreted for President Ikeda's 1974 meeting with Soviet Premier Aleksey Kosygin. He recalls: "The subject matter of the Ikeda-Kosygin meeting was quite different from that normally discussed by Japanese delegations visiting Moscow. They spoke about war and peace, about war and its victims and how to prevent war."[14]

The following January, President Ikeda flew to the United States, where he spoke with leaders who could move the world toward peace. That same month, he traveled to Guam, and there participated in events culminating in the founding of the Soka Gakkai International on January 26. He writes: "The SGI was established in the midst of my efforts to bring the United States, China and the Soviet Union closer together through dialogue in a world shrouded by the dark clouds of the Cold War.

"History teaches us the bitter lesson that coercive balances of power and attempts to resolve conflicts through military force only create greater division. Choosing dialogue is the key to building peace and achieving a victory of our inner humanity.

"Since the founding of the SGI, this truth has continued to ring out vibrantly across the globe as the cry of world citizens."[15]

Former chair of the China-Japan Friendship Association, Sun Pinghua, said of President Ikeda's diplomatic efforts: "The 'golden bridge [of trust]' erected by President Ikeda has a peculiar construction. The more people cross it, the more solid it becomes."[16]

Separation From Nichiren Shoshu

The Soka Gakkai, from its inception in 1930, was the Nichiren Shoshu priesthood's primary benefactor. The Soka Gakkai's growth after World War II transformed Nichiren Shoshu from a poverty-stricken and obscure Buddhist school into one of the largest religious bodies in Japan.

As Soka Gakkai membership grew during the 1970s, President Ikeda began to point out in speeches and lectures that, from the perspective of Nichiren Daishonin's writings, lay believers should in no way be considered inferior to priests. Increasing reports of priests acting in an authoritarian, condescending and even abusive manner toward the laity prompted his actions. Lay members complained of mounting pressure to offer large financial donations to the priests while, at the same time, being treated disrespectfully. President Ikeda tried to engage the priests in dialogue about these concerns.

Many priests felt threatened by his public assertions and his considerable influence. A lawyer for the Soka Gakkai attempted to undermine President Ikeda by exploiting these fears, feeding the priests false reports about the Soka Gakkai's supposed ill intentions. Tensions grew in a climate of accusation and counteraccusation.

In an essay about that intense period, President Ikeda writes: "I agonized over the situation. I knew I had to prevent further suffering from being inflicted on our members and to protect them from the persecution of the priests. Mr. Toda had said that the Soka Gakkai was more precious to him than his own life. The Soka Gakkai is an organization that follows the Buddha's intent and decree to the letter; it is dedicated to the happiness of the people, the propagation of Buddhism and world peace.

"My resolve to take all the blame upon myself and to resign the presidency gradually grew firm within me."[17]

President Ikeda stepped down as president on April 24, 1979. The priesthood set harsh restrictions, forbidding him from addressing Soka Gakkai members at the organization's gatherings and from contributing articles to the organ publications.

Despite these restrictions, he found ways to encourage members. He penned short poems and calligraphy for individuals. He traveled throughout the country, visiting members in their homes. And he took what had seemed a debilitating setback as an opportunity to fulfill an even grander vision—to fortify the SGI and its mission to establish a solid network for building peace throughout the world.

The conflict between the Soka Gakkai and the priesthood eventually seemed to be settled for a time, and President Ikeda, as honorary president of the Soka Gakkai and SGI president, again fulfilled a more public role as a Buddhist leader. In the ensuing years, however, Nikken, the sixty-seventh high priest, conspired to disband the Soka Gakkai or bring it under direct control of the priesthood.

After making public a list of groundless complaints against the lay organization as a pretext, the priesthood refused repeated requests from the Soka Gakkai for dialogue. Unable to win Soka Gakkai members to its side as Nikken had planned, the priesthood excommunicated the entire organization in November 1991.

Nikken had hoped that excommunication would cause large numbers of members to abandon the SGI and follow the priesthood, but only a very small percentage did so. The vast majority remained with the SGI, viewing the excommunication as liberation from an archaic and oppressive institution. The SGI now had the freedom to pursue a more modern and humanistic approach to applying Nichiren Buddhism to the conditions of global society and creating bonds of trust and friendship throughout the world.

Building an Everlasting Foundation for Peace

Daisaku Ikeda, now eighty-five, has continued to pursue dialogue with philosophers, scientists and world leaders, as well as submitting annual peace proposals to the United Nations. Numerous institutions, governments and organizations have acknowledged him as a genuine builder of peace.

He continuously encourages members to develop and strengthen themselves through Buddhist practice so that they may establish happiness and peace in their lives and their communities. And he continues writing daily installments of *The New Human Revolution*, as well as messages, essays and ongoing study series such as "Learning From the Writings of Nichiren Daishonin: The Teachings for Victory." He constantly encourages youth around the world to share the same sense of responsibility he has, to build an everlasting foundation for world peace grounded in the most humane Buddhist principles.

For more than six decades, President Ikeda has kept the vision of his mentor, Josei Toda, close to his heart. He says: "Mr. Toda was focused on the world. He was thinking about humanity as a whole. He once said earnestly: 'Nichiren Buddhism is like the light of the sun. By embracing faith in the Mystic Law, countless Soka Gakkai members have risen up from the depths of despair and vibrantly revitalized their lives.' The Mystic Law makes it possible for humankind to transform its karma. It is here that we find the mission of the Soka Gakkai, an organization dedicated to building peace."[18]

Notes

1. *Tsunesaburo Makiguchi, Education for Creative Living*, edited by Dayle M. Bethel and translated by Alfred Birnbaum (Ames, Iowa: Iowa State University Press, 1994), pp. 5–6.

2. *The Human Revolution*, p. 90.

3. *The Lotus Sutra and Its Opening and Closing Sutras*, p. 178.

4. *The Human Revolution*, p. 1967.

5. See ibid., 232.

6. See ibid., 224–32.

7. Ibid., 529.

8. See ibid., 539–40.

9. Ibid., 563.

10. See ibid., 485–87.

11. Ibid., 1895.

12. Ibid., 1971.

13. *Discussions on Youth*, second edition, p. 169.

14. Kimura, Keiko, *Daisaku Ikeda Up Close* documentary (Owners Promotion, Inc.: Tokyo, 2001).

15. January 1, 2009, *World Tribune*, p. 4

16. Sun, Pinghua, "Meiyo kaicho, chunichi yuko kyokai no Sonheika kaicho to kandan" (President Ikeda's Dialogue With Sun Pinghua, Chair of the China-Japan Friendship Association), July 20, 1990, *Seikyo Shimbun*, p. 1.

17. March–April 2009 *Living Buddhism*, pp. 27–28.

18. March 20, 2009, *World Tribune*, p. 4.

SGI President Ikeda's Study Lecture Series

"The Dragon Gate"

"My Wish Is That All My Disciples Make a Great Vow"—Carrying On the Great Vow for the Happiness of All Humanity

Excerpts From *Learning From the Writings: The Hope-filled Teachings of Nichiren Daishonin*

A waterfall called the Dragon Gate exists in China. Its waters plunge a hundred feet, swifter than an arrow shot by a strong warrior. It is said that a great many carp gather in the basin below, hoping to climb the falls, and that any that succeeds will turn into a dragon. Not a single carp, however, out of a hundred, a thousand, or even ten thousand, can climb the falls, not even after ten or twenty years. Some are swept away by the strong currents, some fall prey to eagles, hawks, kites, and owls, and others are netted, scooped up, or even shot with arrows by fishermen who line both banks of the falls ten *cho* wide. Such is the difficulty a carp faces in becoming a dragon . . .

Attaining Buddhahood is no easier than for men of low status to enter court circles, or for carp to climb the Dragon Gate. Shariputra, for example, practiced bodhisattva austerities for sixty kalpas in order to attain Buddhahood, but finally could persevere no longer and slipped back into the paths of the two vehicles[1] . . .

My wish is that all my disciples make a great vow. (*The Writings of Nichiren Daishonin*, vol. 1, pp. 1002–03)

The Tale of the Dragon Gate

In this letter, Nichiren Daishonin emphasizes that attaining Buddhahood entails overcoming many hurdles and difficulties. To make his point, he draws analogies from the ancient Chinese tale of the Dragon Gate waterfall and the history of the Taira clan in Japan. He also gives an example from the Buddhist scriptures on the difficulty of attaining Buddhahood, citing the story of how Shariputra, one of Shakyamuni's ten major disciples, regressed in his Buddhist practice in a past existence.

Some sources place the legendary Dragon Gate on the upper or middle reaches of the Yellow River. It was held that carp that managed to climb the falls would become dragons. In this letter, the Daishonin describes the Dragon Gate as one hundred feet high and ten *cho* (0.6 miles) wide. In some of his other writings,[2] he describes it as being one thousand feet high and located on Mount T'ien-t'ai.[3] Given these divergences, it is difficult for us to come up with a definitive picture of the falls. Be that as it may, however, the story goes that the force of the current is so intense that most of the carp are unsuccessful in their attempts to climb the falls, no matter how many times they try. Moreover, birds of prey and fishermen lie in wait to catch them. Only a carp that can overcome all these challenges and reach the top of the waterfall can become a dragon with the power to control the rain and thunderclouds. This story is related in the Chinese historical text *The Book of the Later Han*. In many countries in the East to this day, the expression "climbing the Dragon Gate" is used to indicate surmounting difficult hurdles or high barriers to gain success in society or one's profession.

Through this example, Nichiren highlights for [Nanjo] Tokimitsu [to whom this letter was written] that remaining steadfast in one's Buddhist practice to the very end is an undertaking fraught with as many difficulties as a carp faces in climbing the Dragon Gate and turning into a dragon. The strong currents of the waterfall that drive the fish back can be likened to the conditions of an evil age defiled by the five impurities[4] as described in the Lotus Sutra; while the birds of prey and fishermen can be likened to the three obstacles and four devils[5] and the three powerful enemies[6] that hinder one's efforts to attain Buddhahood.

Persevering in faith in the evil age of the Latter Day of the Law is like swimming upstream against a powerful current. It is hard enough just to resist the insidious forces exerted by our own earthly desires and fundamental darkness. Shakyamuni compared these forces to a strong current or flood. Nichiren explains that this is even more true in the Latter Day, when even seemingly remarkable human wisdom and ingenuity can be inundated by an inexorable tide of deluded impulses fueled by the three poisons of greed, anger and foolish-ness—an ever-growing tide that wreaks havoc as a force of evil (see "The Kalpa of Decrease," WND-1, 1121).

Precisely because it is so difficult to carry out faith in the Mystic Law in such an age, the bond of mentor and disciple in Buddhism takes on decisive importance. Likewise, a harmonious community of fellow practitioners solidly united in purpose—in what Nichiren terms "the spirit of many in body, one in mind"—is also indis-pensable. The Soka Gakkai possesses the bond of mentor and disciple that is strong enough to withstand any adversity. And its members—noble ordinary people who are polishing their lives by striving in faith with the same commitment as their mentor—are allied together in solid unity. Moreover, countless members, like magnificent dragons born through the triumphant ascent of the waterfall, are leading lives of profound dignity and confidence forged through continually challenging themselves in their faith and self-development.

(*Learning From the Writings: The Hope-filled Teachings of Nichiren Daishonin*, pp. 119–20)

Be Wary of Negative Influences, or "Evil Friends"

Dragons have the job of making the rain fall—this same work can be regarded as a burden or as a mission, depending on how one looks at it. This difference in outlook or attitude is also what determines whether we will be defeated by negative influences, or evil friends, or successfully attain Buddhahood. Truly, as Nichiren says, "It is the heart that is important" ("The Strategy of the Lotus Sutra," WND-1, 1000). And this difference in heart or spirit comes down to whether or not we embrace the great vow that is mentioned in this letter.

To bring our practice of the Lotus Sutra, or the Mystic Law, to successful completion means that we must eagerly and joyfully embrace the mission of taking on the sufferings of still more and more people and of challenging even greater difficulties in our cause for peace and happiness. Nichiren urges us to actively seek this way of life, to valiantly climb the Dragon Gate of faith as successors of kosen-rufu, and attain Buddhahood without fail. As practitioners of the Mystic Law, this is what it means for us to "live based on a great vow."

(*Learning From the Writings: The Hope-filled Teachings of Nichiren Daishonin*, p. 125)

Notes

1. This story is found in *The Treatise on Great Perfection of Wisdom*. Once, when Shariputra was engaged in offering alms as part of his bodhisattva practice in a previous existence, a Brahman begged him for his eye. Shariputra gave it to him, but the Brahman was so revolted by its smell that he dropped it on the ground and trampled on it. Seeing this, Shariputra discontinued his bodhisattva practice, retreating into the Hinayana teachings, or the way of voice-hearers, and failed to attain Buddhahood (see "The Dragon Gate," WND-1, 1004).

2. See "Letter to Akimoto," WND-1, 1021, and "Climbing Up Dragon Gate," WND-2, 673.

3. Mount T'ien-t'ai: A mountain in Zhejiang Province in China where the Great Teacher T'ien-t'ai lived and where the T'ien-t'ai school was based. Mount T'ien-t'ai prospered as a center of Chinese Buddhism, and a number of temples were built there.

4. Five impurities: Also, five defilements. "Expedient Means," the second chapter of the Lotus Sutra, says, "The Buddhas appear in evil worlds of five impurities . . . In this evil world of the five impurities those who merely delight in and are attached to the desires, living beings such as this in the end will never seek the Buddha way." (1) Impurity of the age includes repeated disruptions of the social or natural environment. (2) Impurity of desire is the tendency to be ruled by the five delusive inclinations (greed, anger, foolishness, arrogance and doubt). (3) Impurity of living beings is the physical and spiritual decline of human beings. (4) Impurity of thought, or impurity of view, is the prevalence of wrong views such as the five false views. (5) Impurity of life span is the shortening of the life spans of living beings. According to *The Words and Phrases of the Lotus Sutra,* the most fundamental of these five are the impurities of thought and desire, which result in the impurity of living beings and the impurity of life span. These in turn give rise to the impurity of the age.

5. Three obstacles and four devils: Various obstacles and hindrances to the practice of Buddhism. The three obstacles are (1) the obstacle of earthly desires, (2) the obstacle of karma and (3) the obstacle of retribution. The four devils are (1) the hindrance of the five components, (2) the hindrance of earthly desires, (3) the hindrance of death and (4) the hindrance of the devil king.

6. Three powerful enemies: Also, three types of enemies. Three types of arrogant people who persecute those who propagate the Lotus Sutra in the evil age after Shakyamuni Buddha's death. Miao-lo summarizes these three as follows: (1) "The arrogance and presumption of lay people" or arrogant lay people; a reference to those ignorant of Buddhism who curse and speak ill of the practitioners of the Lotus Sutra and attack them with swords and staves. (2) "The arrogance and presumption of members of the Buddhist clergy" or arrogant priests. These are priests with perverse wisdom and hearts that are fawning and crooked who, though failing to understand Buddhism, boast they have attained the Buddhist truth and slander the sutra's practitioners. (3) "The arrogance and presumption of those who pretend to be sages" or arrogant false sages. This third category is described as priests who pretend to be sages and who are revered as such, but when encountering the practitioners of the Lotus Sutra become fearful of losing fame or profit and induce secular authorities to persecute them.

"How Those Initially Aspiring to the Way Can Attain Buddhahood through the Lotus Sutra"

The Vibrant Chanting of Nam-myoho-renge-kyo Is the Driving Force for Limitless Progress—Everything Starts With Our Own Inner Transformation

Excerpts from *The Writings of Nichiren Daishonin: The Teachings for Victory*

When we revere Myoho-renge-kyo inherent in our own life as the object of devotion, the Buddha nature within us is summoned forth and manifested by our chanting of Nam-myoho-renge-kyo. This is what is meant by "Buddha." To illustrate, when a caged bird sings, birds who are flying in the sky are thereby summoned and gather around, and when the birds flying in the sky gather around, the bird in the cage strives to get out. When with our mouths we chant the Mystic Law, our Buddha nature, being summoned, will invariably emerge. The Buddha nature of Brahma and Shakra, being called, will protect us, and the Buddha nature of the Buddhas and bodhisattvas, being summoned, will rejoice. This is what the Buddha meant when he said, "If one can uphold it [the Mystic Law] even for a short while I will surely rejoice and so will the other Buddhas."[1] (*The Writings of Nichiren Daishonin*, vol. 1, p. 887)

Establishing a State of Indestructible Happiness

Here, Nichiren Daishonin describes the great benefits of chanting Nam-myoho- renge-kyo, the single sound with which we can summon forth the Buddha nature of all living beings.

He begins by speaking of revering "Myoho-renge-kyo inherent in our own life as the object of devotion" (WND-1, 887). The Daishonin revealed the Mystic Law inherent in his own life and manifested it in the concrete form of the Gohonzon, the object of devotion or fundamental respect. Only when our chanting of Nam-myoho-renge-kyo is based on faith in the Gohonzon does it become a practice for attaining Buddhahood.

We revere the Gohonzon bestowed on humanity by Nichiren, taking it as a mirror and guide for our life, and believe that we possess and can manifest within us the same supremely noble state of life as the Daishonin. By doing so, we are revering "Myoho-renge-kyo inherent in our own life as the object of devotion" (WND-1, 887).

The Daishonin—embodying the three virtues of sovereign, teacher and parent[2]— strove with boundless compassion in a dark and evil age to protect and teach people, and help them reveal their highest potential. The way for us to show true reverence and respect for the Gohonzon is to venerate the Daishonin as our fundamental mentor or teacher in faith, learn from his selfless dedication, and carry on his efforts for the happiness and welfare of all people.

In other words, to revere the Gohonzon essentially means that, no matter how troubled the times, we strive to make our mentor's spirit our own, take personal action for kosen-rufu, and become a source of hope, courage and peace of mind for others.

We are not truly revering "Myoho-renge-kyo inherent in our own life as the object of devotion" (WND-1, 887) if we seek the assistance of, or put our faith in, some supernatural being or Buddha outside of our own lives to attain salvation—for example, like one of the Buddhas taught in the provisional, pre-Lotus Sutra teachings,[3] as is the case in the Nembutsu faith.

In "The Real Aspect of the Gohonzon," Nichiren writes: "Never seek this Gohonzon outside yourself. The Gohonzon exists only within the mortal flesh of us ordinary people who embrace the Lotus Sutra and chant Nam-myoho-renge-kyo"(WND-1, 832). When the Daishonin embodied his own Buddhahood, "the soul of Nichiren" ("Reply to Kyo'o," WND-1, 412), in the form of the mandala that is the Gohonzon, his purpose was to enable each of us to reveal the Gohonzon that exists within us. The Gohonzon is the clear mirror that enables us to manifest the Gohonzon in our own life.

Chanting with faith in the Gohonzon is the key to manifesting the Gohonzon within us and activating the "Myoho-renge-kyo inherent in our own life" (WND-1, 887). If we were to lose sight of this important point, our Buddhist practice runs the risk of lapsing into the subservient worship of some absolute being outside of us.

My mentor, second Soka Gakkai president Josei Toda, often said: "You yourself are Nam-myoho-renge-kyo"; and "How can a Buddha be defeated by illness or economic hardship?" Once we awaken to our enormous potential, we can face any adversity. The purpose of faith in Nichiren Buddhism is to develop such inner strength.

Out of a spirit of profound compassion, Mr. Toda often gave strict guidance to members who lacked conviction in faith and displayed a resigned or defeatist attitude. When those same members later came back to share with him their experiences of overcoming difficulties and achieving victory in their lives, he would smile happily and rejoice together with them on their success. He constantly urged people to awaken to their greater self and to reveal their true potential.

The purpose of our Buddhist practice is for each of us to bring forth the "Myoho-renge-kyo inherent in our own life" (WND-1, 887) and establish an inner state of everlasting and indestructible happiness.

When We Chant, Our Life Communes
With the Universe

In this letter, Nichiren Daishonin writes: "When we revere Myoho-renge-kyo inherent in our own life as the object of devotion [Gohonzon], the Buddha nature within us is summoned forth and manifested by our chanting of Nam-myoho-renge-kyo. This is what is meant by 'Buddha'" (WND-1, 887).

He then proceeds to explain the process by which this great life state of Buddhahood manifests, employing the very accessible metaphor of a bird in a cage: "When a caged bird sings, birds who are flying in the sky are thereby summoned and gather around, and when the birds flying in the sky gather around, the bird in the cage strives to get out" (WND-1, 887).

The "bird in the cage" represents the Buddha nature of us ordinary people. The cage represents a state of being shackled by fundamental darkness or ignorance, various deluded impulses or earthly desires, and all kinds of suffering. The "caged bird sings" refers to ordinary people rousing faith in the Mystic Law and chanting Nam-myoho-renge-kyo. The "birds who are flying in the sky," meanwhile, represent the Buddha nature of all living beings. We call forth our Buddha nature—that is, the Myoho-renge-kyo within us—by chanting with our own voices.

At the same time, however, the sound of our chanting in fact also calls forth the Buddha nature of diverse living beings. This is because—as we saw in the earlier passage—Myoho-renge-kyo is also the name of the Buddha nature of all Buddhas, bodhisattvas and other living beings in the Ten Worlds. Once we chant the Mystic Law, therefore, its power is such that it can call forth the Buddha nature of all of them. In other words, our voice chanting Nam-myoho-renge-kyo is the powerful sound that awakens and summons forth the Buddha nature of all living beings throughout the universe.

When the birds flying in the sky are called forth by the bird in the cage and gather around it, the bird in the cage tries to get out, says the Daishonin. The moment when the cage of ignorance and suffering disappears, we are liberated from all shackles of illusion, and can soar freely in "the sky of the essential nature of phenomena"[4] ("On the Large Carriages Drawn by White Oxen," WND-2, 976)—that is, the realm of enlightenment as vast and unimpeded as the heavens.

Earnest prayer in the form of chanting Nam-myoho-renge-kyo resonates with the Mystic Law that pervades the universe, envelops one's own life and brings forth the power to break through one's own inner darkness or ignorance. In other words, the act of chanting Nam-myoho-renge-kyo is a drama of profound communion or interaction between ourselves and the universe.

(February 2012 *Living Buddhism*, pp. 25–28)

Notes

1. *The Lotus Sutra and Its Opening and Closing Sutras*, p. 220.

2. Three virtues of sovereign, teacher and parent: Three benevolent functions that a Buddha is said to possess. The virtue of the sovereign is the power to protect all living beings, the virtue of the teacher is the wisdom to instruct and lead them to enlightenment, and the virtue of the parent is the compassion to nurture and support them.

3. The provisional teachings that precede the Lotus Sutra do not teach that the world of Buddhahood exists in all people, and instead describe Buddhas as idealized and superior beings. The Pure Land (Nembutsu) teachings, for example, explain that instead of relying on one's own efforts, one should exclusively depend on salvation through such a Buddha—namely, Amida.

4. "The sky of the essential nature of phenomena": Refers to the fundamental nature of enlightenment. Also, Dharma nature. The unchanging nature inherent in all things and phenomena. It is identified with the fundamental Law itself, the essence of the Buddha's enlightenment, or ultimate truth.

"The Real Aspect of the Gohonzon"

Tapping the Infinite Benefit of the Gohonzon Through Faith

Excerpts from *The Writings of Nichiren Daishonin: The Teachings for Victory*

Never seek this Gohonzon outside yourself. The Gohonzon exists only within the mortal flesh of us ordinary people who embrace the Lotus Sutra and chant Nam-myoho-renge-kyo. The body is the palace of the ninth consciousness,[1] the unchanging reality that reigns over all of life's functions. To be endowed with the Ten Worlds means that all ten, without a single exception, exist in one world. Because of this it is called a mandala. Mandala is a Sanskrit word that is translated as "perfectly endowed" or "a cluster of blessings." This Gohonzon also is found only in the two characters for faith.[2] This is what the sutra means when it states that one can "gain entrance through faith alone."[3] (*The Writings of Nichiren Daishonin*, vol. 1, p. 832)

The Gohonzon Exists Within Us

Nichinyo must have been extremely moved to learn that the Gohonzon she received from Nichiren Daishonin is the Gohonzon that has been revealed for the first time in the Latter Day of the Law. But, then, he discloses an even more astonishing fact, writing: "Never seek this Gohonzon outside yourself. The Gohonzon exists only within the mortal flesh of us ordinary people who embrace the Lotus Sutra and chant Nam-myoho-renge-kyo" (WND-1, 832). He is saying that the Gohonzon does not exist outside us, but within our own lives. Shifting the focus of faith and practice from the external to the internal was a dramatic change.

In Nichiren's day—and, in many cases, even today—we find a deeply rooted view that we are but small, insignificant beings and the ultimate reality and eternal value lies somewhere outside of us, somewhere far away. Such a way of thinking is inextricably connected with belief in some otherworldly, supernatural power.

Nichiren Buddhism, however, rejects this idea completely. It teaches the true reality of life in which the eternal and ultimate Law is manifested in the physical beings of the ordinary people, living right here and now.

The term *Buddha*, after all, means "enlightened one." To what did the Buddha become enlightened? To that which should form the true basis of our life—namely, the Law and the true essence of our being. He awoke to the universal Law permeating all phenomena, which had previously been obscured by fundamental darkness,[4] and to the greatness of each individual's life that is one and indivisible with that Law.

"The Gohonzon exists only within the mortal flesh of us ordinary people"—the real significance of this statement is that the Gohonzon inscribed by Nichiren functions as the means by which we can awaken to and call forth the Gohonzon (the Buddhahood) within us. When we chant before the physical Gohonzon, the very same Gohonzon is in our heart; it clearly manifests itself there when we chant Nam-myoho-renge-kyo for the happiness of ourselves and others.

In another letter that the Daishonin sent to Nichinyo the following year (1278), titled "An Outline of the 'Entrustment' and Other Chapters," he writes in a similar vein, "When I ponder where this 'Treasure Tower' chapter is now, I see that it exists in the eight-petaled lotus flower of the heart[5] within the breast of Nichinyo" (WND-1, 915). No doubt when she read the Daishonin's words, Nichinyo was reminded of his earlier assertion that "the Gohonzon exists only within the mortal flesh of us ordinary people." Here, the terms "within the mortal flesh" and "in the eight-petaled lotus flower of the heart" have the same meaning of "within the depths of one's own life."

Still another way Nichiren describes our inner being is "the palace of the ninth consciousness, the unchanging reality that reigns over all of life's functions" (WND-1, 832). The ninth consciousness—also the *amala*-consciousness, or pure consciousness—is often referred to in Buddhist texts as the "mind king"[6] or "ruler of the mind," indicating the fundamental entity of the mind itself. "The unchanging reality" means the ultimate truth, free from all delusion. Since the "mind king" dwells in this unchanging reality, our mortal bodies are called its "palace."

In "Reply to Kyo'o," he writes, "I, Nichiren, have inscribed my life in sumi ink, so believe in the Gohonzon with your whole heart" (WND-1, 412). He is saying here that he has inscribed in the form of the Gohonzon the life state of Buddhahood that he has attained as a votary of the Lotus Sutra, a life state that is identical with the unchanging reality.

The Gohonzon is in the form of a mandala. The Sanskrit term *mandala* has also been translated into Chinese as "perfectly endowed" and "a cluster of blessings" (see WND-1, 832). It means a trove of infinite benefit that we can draw from and enjoy freely.

Mr. Toda said, "Nichiren Daishonin's life is Nam-myoho-renge-kyo, so our lives, as his disciples, are also Nam-myoho-renge-kyo."[7]

On another occasion, he declared: "When we embrace faith in the Mystic Law, the fundamental power of Nichiren Daishonin wells up in response from within our beings, and we, too, reveal our true self—that is, our true enlightened nature that is one with the eternal, unchanging reality."[8]

(September 2012 *Living Buddhism*, pp. 29–31)

Notes

1. Ninth consciousness: Also, *amala*-consciousness. The Buddha nature, or the fundamental purifying force, that is free from all karmic impediments. Here, the Daishonin is associating it with Nam-myoho-renge-kyo.

2. The Japanese word *faith* consists of two Chinese characters.

3. *The Lotus Sutra and Its Opening and Closing Sutras*, p. 110.

4. Fundamental darkness: The most deeply rooted illusion inherent in life, said to give rise to all other illusions. The inability to see or recognize the truth, particularly, the true nature of one's life.

5. The "eight-petaled lotus flower of the heart" refers to the arrangement of the heart, lungs and other organs in the chest cavity, which was thought to resemble an eight-petaled lotus blossom.

6. The "mind king" refers to the core of the mind, which controls the various workings of the mind.

7. Translated from Japanese. Josei Toda, *Toda Josei zenshu* (The Collected Writings of Josei Toda) (Tokyo: Seikyo Shimbunsha, 1985), vol. 5, p. 271.

8. Translated from Japanese. Josei Toda, *Toda Josei zenshu* (The Collected Writings of Josei Toda) (Tokyo: Seikyo Shimbunsha, 1992), vol. 2, p. 11.

Soka Spirit

Three Key Errors of the Nichiren Shoshu Priesthood

Tsunesaburo Makiguchi and Josei Toda, the first two presidents of the Soka Gakkai, began their Buddhist practice as lay members of Nichiren Shoshu. That was the twentieth-century name of the Buddhist order founded in the thirteenth century by Nikko Shonin, Nichiren Daishonin's closest disciple and immediate successor.

Originally known as the Fuji school, Nichiren Shoshu had unfortunately dwindled to become one of Japan's smaller and impoverished Buddhist schools, having long since lost its founding spirit to accomplish kosen-rufu—to widely propagate the law of Nam-myoho-renge-kyo that Nichiren taught. Nevertheless, Makiguchi, an educator devoted to scholastic reform, deeply studied Nichiren's writings, and thereby awoke to the profound power of Nichiren's teachings to revitalize the lives of ordinary people and society. He awakened in himself a personal vow to accomplish kosen-rufu as a disciple of Nichiren Daishonin, a vow that Makiguchi's disciple, Josei Toda, shared.

Based on the staunch faith and sense of mission of the founding presidents, the Soka Gakkai quickly grew into a dynamic, progressive and socially engaged lay Buddhist movement. For decades, the Soka Gakkai gave wholehearted support to the Nichiren Shoshu priesthood, building hundreds of new temples and completely restoring its head temple, Taiseki-ji. At the same time, the Soka Gakkai struggled to maintain a harmonious relationship with the priesthood, which had become overwhelmingly authoritarian and ritualistic.

From the beginning, the two had conflicting priorities. The priests of Nichiren Shoshu were focused on maintaining their order and its traditions. The Soka Gakkai was focused on realizing Nichiren's vow to accomplish kosen-rufu, the widespread propagation of his teachings for the peace and happiness of humankind.

Prior to the Soka Gakkai, as with most Buddhist denominations in Japan, most lay believers of Nichiren Shoshu did not carry out a daily Buddhist practice. Priests were expected to recite the sutra and conduct rites such as funerals and memorials on the laity's behalf.

President Makiguchi was the first to propose a format for chanting Nam-myoho-renge-kyo together with reciting the Lotus Sutra as part of the daily practice of lay believers. The appearance of a proactive laity that embraced the mission to accomplish kosen-rufu was a major departure from the passive approach Nichiren Shoshu believers had long taken.

By the 1970s and 1980s, Nichiren Shoshu had become wealthy through the generous donations and support of the Soka Gakkai members. The Soka Gakkai and its international movement, the SGI, continued to grow. But the open, engaged and dynamic movement triggered growing resentment among certain priests of Nichiren Shoshu. Their worldview was rooted in centuries of Japanese Buddhist history in which lay believers were seen as passive participants, whose role it was simply to venerate and make donations to the priests. Of course, this was not the view of Nichiren Daishonin, who treasured and fully empowered his lay followers. But to the priesthood, the dynamic SGI, in which laity took the initiative in an atmosphere of mutual encouragement, represented a threat.

A few of the senior priests, including a priest called Nikken, who would become the sixty-seventh high priest, became intensely jealous and vindictive toward the Soka Gakkai and its president, Daisaku Ikeda, who had consistently been dedicated to supporting the priesthood and enhancing its prosperity. This jealousy became what Buddhism describes as a devilish function, turning priests who should have been celebrating and supporting the great progress of kosen-rufu into those bent on destroying it.

In early 1991, under the direction of its high priest, Nikken, the priesthood launched a series of measures to disband the Soka Gakkai. Finally, in November 1991, they issued an order excommunicating the organization, aiming to prompt a large percentage of Soka Gakkai members to leave the organization and directly join their temples.

That didn't happen.

The crux of the priesthood's motives lay in its view that priests are necessary intermediaries between lay believers and the power and teachings of Nichiren Buddhism. Emphasizing ritual and formality not found in Nichiren Daishonin's writings, the priests sought to make veneration and obedience to themselves and their high priest, in particular, the most important aspect of a practitioner's faith.

In contrast, the Soka Gakkai bases itself directly on the spirit and intent of Nichiren Daishonin as set forth in his writings and proven in practice by the organization's founding presidents. The fact that the SGI has flourished all the more since the time of its excommunication is evidence of its correct interpretation and practice of Nichiren's teachings. SGI members in 192 countries and territories have consistently proven the power of correct faith and practice of Nichiren Buddhism in their lives and in their communities.

The following three points summarize the roots of the errors of the Nichiren Shoshu priesthood.

Error 1: The Absolute Power of the High Priest

"Faith in the high priest" has become the central doctrine of Nichiren Shoshu, which has incorrectly elevated the position of the chief priest of their head temple to that of the object of worship. The priesthood upholds the view that, without venerating and obediently following the high priest, practitioners cannot attain enlightenment—a view that undermines the self-empowering properties of Nichiren Buddhism and contradicts the writings of Nichiren Daishonin.

According to the priesthood, the high priest alone has the power to determine who attains Buddhahood and who does not. They write, "The master gives his sanction to a disciple's enlightenment . . . The very establishment of the object of worship according to the sanction of the High Priest, who is the only person to be bequeathed the Daishonin's Buddhism, is what makes the attainment of Buddhahood possible."[1]

The idea of the high priest "sanctioning" a disciple's enlightenment is found nowhere in the teachings of Nichiren Daishonin. Nor does the concept of the high priest being absolute and infallible originate in Nichiren's teachings. Rather, these concepts appeared centuries after Nichiren in order to bolster the status of the office of high priest of the Fuji school at times when those holding the office lacked the respect and support of the other priests.

Nichiren's successor, Nikko Shonin, states in his "Twenty-six Admonitions," "Do not follow even the high priest if he goes against the Buddha's Law and propounds his own views" (*Gosho zenshu*, p. 1618).[2] It is obvious that Nikko did not consider those who would hold the office of high priest to be beyond the possibility of error or corruption. Having absolute faith in whoever holds the office of the high priest is an erroneous teaching completely contrary to what Nichiren taught.

Error 2: The High Priest Receives Exclusive Transmission of the Law

To justify the notion that the high priest is absolute, the priesthood propounds the mysterious idea of the "heritage of the Law being entrusted to a single person."[3] In other words, they encourage "single-minded faith in [the high priest] as the living body of Shakyamuni (Nichiren)"[4] through which practitioners can access the heritage of the Law.

They state that the transmission takes place through a "golden utterance" in a face-to-face conversation between the outgoing high priest and his successor and that "the fundamental principle of the Daishonin's Buddhism is transmitted only to the High Priest."[5]

Quite to the contrary, Nichiren repeatedly stresses that the Law is inherited through embracing the Gohonzon with faith. He states: "The heritage of the Lotus Sutra flows within the lives of those who never forsake it . . .

"Nichiren has been trying to awaken all the people of Japan to faith in the Lotus Sutra so that they too can share the heritage and attain Buddhahood" ("The Heritage of the Ultimate Law of Life," *The Writings of Nichiren Daishonin*, vol. 1, p. 217).

The idea of an exclusive lineage belonging to a select group of clergy was prevalent in other Buddhist schools during the Daishonin's time, but Nichiren himself took pains to refute such views in his writings. Concerning the question of who controls what is holy or sacred in the universe and the human heart, Nichiren Buddhism teaches that all people have equal access through their own faith and practice.

Error 3: Inequality of Priests and Laity

That priests are afforded an elevated status in society is especially true in Japan. During the seventeenth century, partly in response to the influx of Christianity, the Japanese government mandated that all citizens register with their local Buddhist temple. Priests became de facto agents of the government, conducting the census, issuing travel and work documents, and becoming intertwined in both the secular and religious lives of the people.

Nichiren Shoshu states: "Nichiren Shoshu believers must support their direct masters, who are the chief priests of their local temples, and offer their devotion to the major master, who is the High Priest."[6]

In his letter to the Soka Gakkai on January 12, 1991, Nichijun Fujimoto, the general administrator of Nichiren Shoshu, wrote: "To talk about the priesthood and the laity with a sense of equality manifests great conceit. In fact, it corresponds to the five cardinal sins—to destroy the unity of Buddhist practitioners."

And more recently, the priesthood published, "It is only natural that an innate difference exists between the priesthood and laity in the Daishonin's Buddhism."[7]

Nichiren clarifies the equality of priests and laity when he states: "The Buddha surely considers anyone in this world who embraces the Lotus Sutra, whether lay man or woman, monk or nun, to be the lord of all living beings" ("The Unity of Husband and Wife," WND-1, 463); and "Anyone who teaches others even a single phrase of the Lotus Sutra is the envoy of the Thus Come One, whether that person be priest or layman, nun or laywoman" ("A Ship to Cross the Sea of Suffering," WND-1, 33).

And finally, he writes: "Shakyamuni Buddha who attained enlightenment countless kalpas ago, the Lotus Sutra that leads all people to Buddhahood, and we ordinary human beings are in no way different or separate from one another. To chant Myoho-renge-kyo with this realization is to inherit the ultimate Law of life and death. This is a matter of the utmost importance for Nichiren's disciples and lay supporters, and this is what it means to embrace the Lotus Sutra" ("The Heritage of the Ultimate Law of Life," WND-1, 216).

The equality of all people is a fundamental tenet of the Lotus Sutra and Nichiren Buddhism. The correct relationship between a Buddhist teacher and a disciple is expressed in the principle of the oneness of mentor and disciple, which means that both the teacher and the disciple equally share responsibility for kosen-rufu based on mutual respect and commitment. A genuine teacher becomes qualified as such through relentless struggle to awaken Buddhahood within ordinary people in the face of all obstacles, even at the risk of one's own life.

But in Nichiren Shoshu, the teacher is qualified simply by office and rank. Rather than selflessly working to teach others, the high priest requires that others venerate him, while considering lay believers unworthy to know the "secrets" he supposedly possesses. It is important that we clearly understand that this approach is a distortion of Buddhism and seek to develop a correct understanding through our study and practice of the principles Nichiren himself taught.

Notes

1. *A Refutation of the Soka Gakkai's "Counterfeit Object of Worship": 100 Questions and Answers* (Los Angeles: Nichiren Shoshu Temple, 1996), p. 8.

2. See *The Untold History of the Fuji School* (Santa Monica, California: World Tribune Press, 2000), p. 21.

3. *Nichiren Shoshu Monthly*, October 2008 (Los Angeles: Nichiren Shoshu Temple, 2008), p. 17.

4. *Nichiren Shoshu Monthly*, September 2008, p. 22.

5. *Nichiren Shoshu Monthly*, December 2008, p. 21.

6. *Nichiren Shoshu Monthly*, March 2009, p. 8.

7. *Nichiren Shoshu Monthly*, February 2009, p. 22.